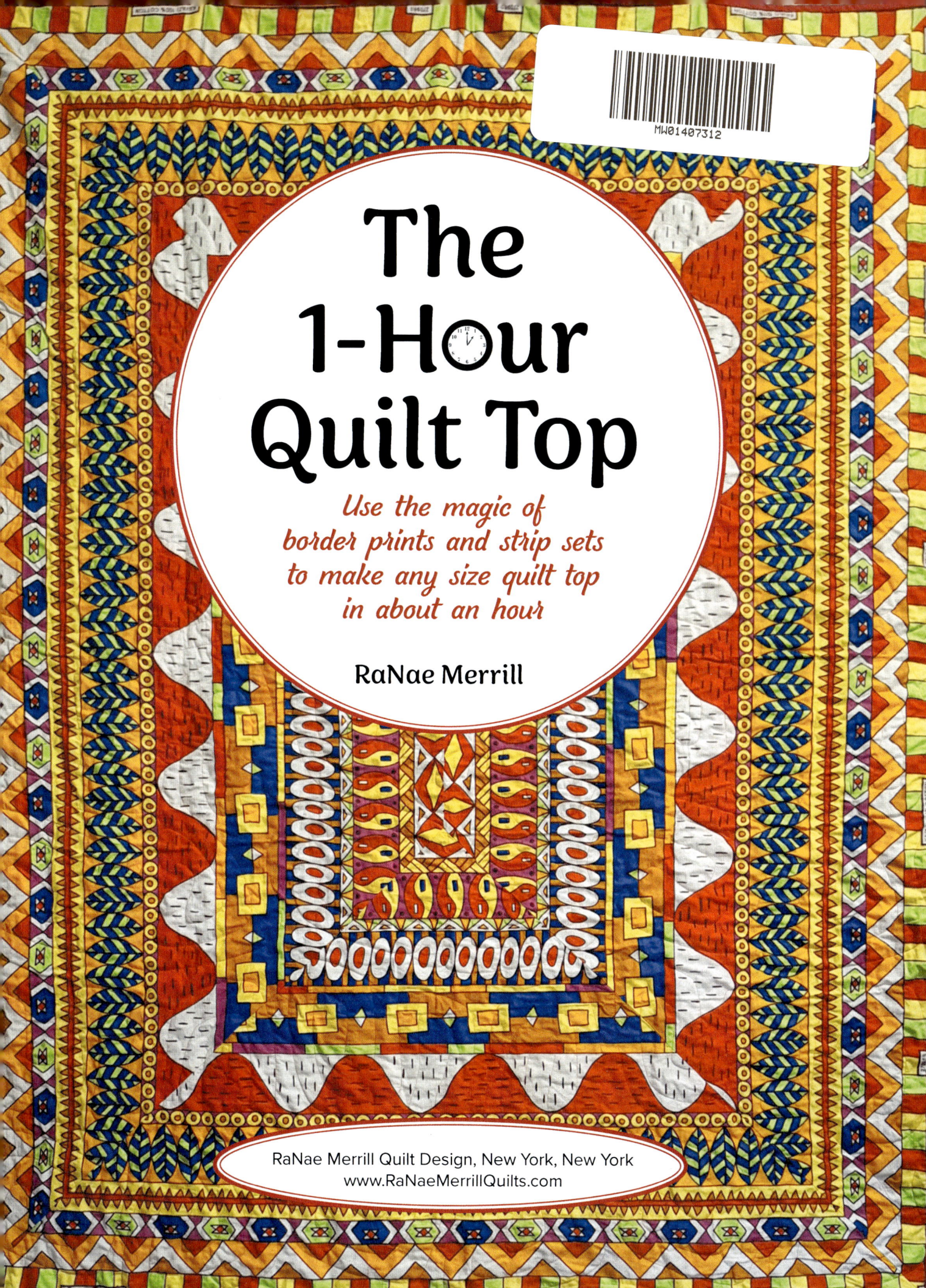

The 1-Hour Quilt Top

Use the magic of border prints and strip sets to make any size quilt top in about an hour

RaNae Merrill

RaNae Merrill Quilt Design, New York, New York
www.RaNaeMerrillQuilts.com

The 1-Hour Quilt Top
Copyright © 2025 by RaNae Merrill

ISBN: 978-1-942853-14-5

PUBLISHED BY
RaNae Merrill Quilt Design
370 West 118th Street #2D
New York, NY 10026
www.RaNaeMerrillQuilts.com
Info@RaNaeMerrillQuilts.com

COVER/BOOK DESIGN: RaNae Merrill
PHOTOGRAPHY: RaNae Merrill
ILLUSTRATION: RaNae Merrill

Manufactured in the United States
All rights reserved

Charts in this book are for the personal use of the reader. By permission of the author and publisher, they may be photocopied to make single copies for personal use by the book owner, but under no circumstances may they be resold, republished or used for teaching. No other part of this book may be reproduced in any form or by any electronic or mechanical means including information storage and retrieval systems without permission in writing from the publisher, except by a reviewer who may quote brief passages in a review.

NO AI TRAINING: Without in any way limiting the author's and publisher's exclusive rights under copyright, any use of this publication to "train" generative artificial intelligence (AI) technologies to generate text is expressly prohibited. The author reserves all rights to license uses of this work for generative AI training and development of machine learning language models.

2025.1

AVAILABLE AT

www.RaNaeMerrillQuilts.com
www.Amazon.com

Quilt on Front Cover by RaNae Merrill
Quilts on Back Cover by RaNae Merrill

Meet RaNae!

If you had told me 20 years ago that I would make my living as a quilter, I wouldn't have believed you. Quilting found me and has given me the great joy of sharing creativity with other people for the better part of two decades.

One of the things I have found most surprising in this time is how so much of what I learned in my previous careers — pianist, photographer, travel writer — applies to what I do today. Teaching young children in music classes led to the unique approach to free-motion quilting in Free-Motion Mastery in a Month. Attention to detail from reading music helps ensure that my patterns are accurate. And so much more!

But the thing I find most gratifying in all of this is that moment when a student "gets it" or when they hold up something beautiful they just created and smile with satisfaction. I hope this book brings you that kind of joy.

When I'm not quilting and writing, you can find me outdoors hiking, kayaking, skiing and golfing, or indoors playing the piano and cooking.

I live in New York City, just north of Central Park.

Table of Contents

Thanks & Introduction 4, 5

What Is a 1-Hour Quilt Top? 7

That's What I'm Talkin' About! Terms to Know 8

Border Prints: The Star of the Show! 11
    Repeats 12
    Symmetry 14
    Finding & Auditioning Border Prints 18

Strip Sets: The Supporting Cast 19
    Strip Set Structure 20
    Building Your Strip Set 23

Patterns 25
    About the Standard Patterns 26
    Tools & Batting 27
    Techniques 28
    Preparing the Mother Strip 32
    • **Rectangle Box Quilt** 35
        Half & Half Construction 38
        Y-Seam Construction 44
    • **Square Box Quilt** 49
    • **Diamond-in-the-Square Quilt** 57
    • **Stripe Quilt** 63

Quilting 64
    Backing Yardage Chart 68

Binding 66

Tools for Building Strip Sets 69
    Strip Set Planning Chart 70
    Component Set Yardage Chart 72
    Sample Quilts 75
    Mother Strip Length Inches to Yards Conversion Chart 80

Resources 81

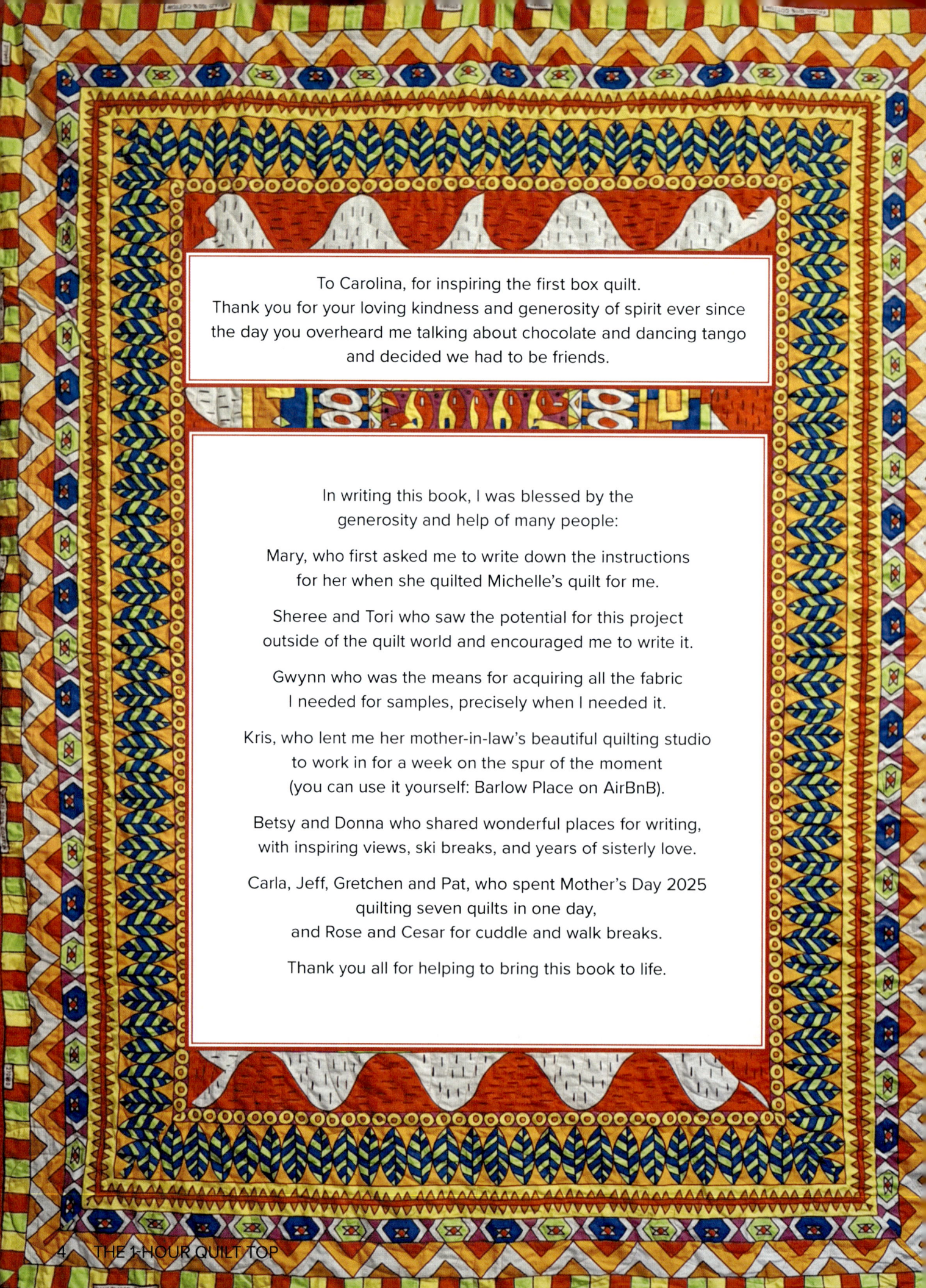

To Carolina, for inspiring the first box quilt.
Thank you for your loving kindness and generosity of spirit ever since the day you overheard me talking about chocolate and dancing tango and decided we had to be friends.

In writing this book, I was blessed by the
generosity and help of many people:

Mary, who first asked me to write down the instructions
for her when she quilted Michelle's quilt for me.

Sheree and Tori who saw the potential for this project
outside of the quilt world and encouraged me to write it.

Gwynn who was the means for acquiring all the fabric
I needed for samples, precisely when I needed it.

Kris, who lent me her mother-in-law's beautiful quilting studio
to work in for a week on the spur of the moment
(you can use it yourself: Barlow Place on AirBnB).

Betsy and Donna who shared wonderful places for writing,
with inspiring views, ski breaks, and years of sisterly love.

Carla, Jeff, Gretchen and Pat, who spent Mother's Day 2025
quilting seven quilts in one day,
and Rose and Cesar for cuddle and walk breaks.

Thank you all for helping to bring this book to life.

1-Hour Quilts: How it all began...

When my dear friend Carolina got married several years ago (more than I care to admit now!), I asked her what colors she wanted in a quilt. Her answer: "Orange, purple and blue." I thought "UGH!" but I love her and so I went to my stash to see what fabrics I had. I found a lot of oranges that had languished for a while. I paired them up with purples and blues to make a strip set that I then cut into triangles and trapezoids to make this quilt. I liked it way more than I expected to — and she loves it to this day. In fact, each year when I go to Houston for Quilt Festival, she hosts me and I get to curl up on the couch with this quilt (sometimes accompanied by her dog, Riott). I thought then that the idea of a box quilt might be a good idea for a book someday

Fast forward a few years . . . I found an unusually exuberant, colorful, striped fabric at an African fabric shop near my home in NYC. I immediately

Carolina's wedding quilt

Michelle's college quilt

thought of one of my nieces — a cheerful, outgoing girl — and bought a 10-yard length to make a going-away-to-college quilt. I used the box quilt idea again, and the fabric actually made three quilts (you can see them on pages 34 and 62). They were really fast and easy to make, and the idea of a box quilt book was revived.

I have lots of nieces and nephews, and over the years I have come to realize that the best quilts for them were ones that they could use without fear of ruining them. If a quilt gets "loved to death" no one feels bad and I can easily replace it. So, I started making them quilts that are fast and easy, yet still beautiful. One-hour quilts fit the bill perfectly!

And now, here's the book!

HOW IT ALL BEGAN

Four 1-Hour Quilt Tops

Rectangle Box
Make two "sister" quilts at once

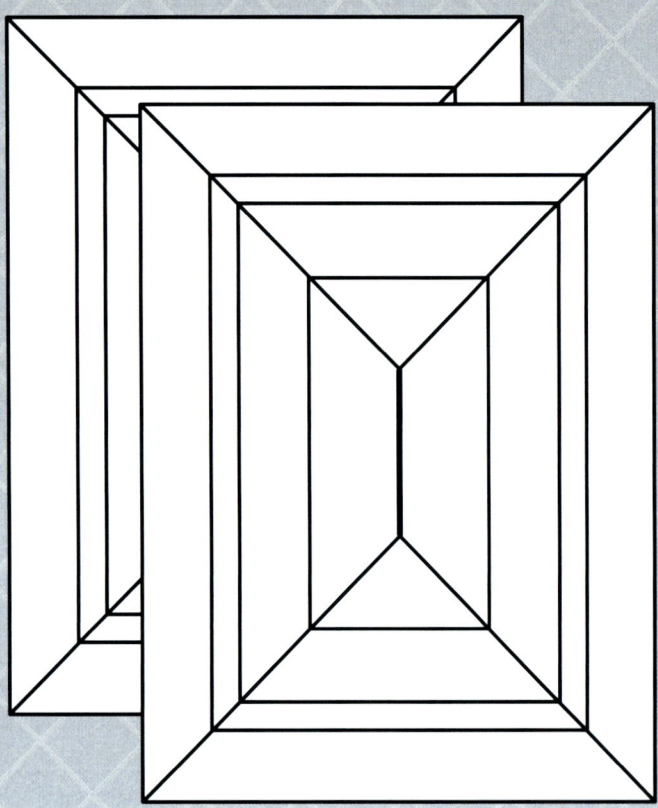

Diamond-in-the-Square
Make one or two quilts at once

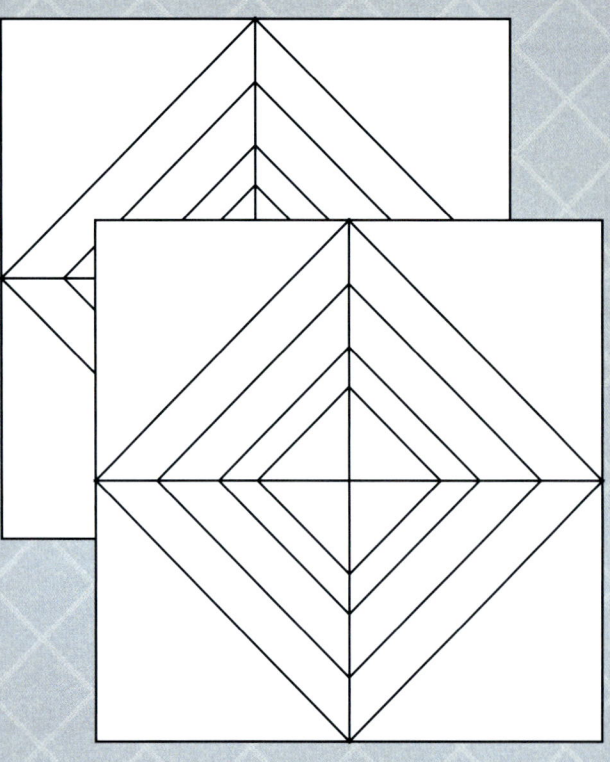

Square Box
Make two quilts at once

Stripe
Make one quilt top (or back) from the fabric left after making the box quilts above

What is a 1-Hour Quilt Top?

A quilt top made from border prints or a strip set that you can assemble quickly and easily in about an hour. The quilts can be rectangular, square, diamond-in-a-square, or stripe, and they can be any size.

One-hour quilt tops use the power of border print fabrics to create the quilt design for you. Start with several yards of fabric, or build a strip set, then make a few simple cuts, rearrange the pieces, and assemble them with a few seams. The process makes up to three quilt tops at once. Each top takes about an hour. (Yes, really. Even if you are a complete beginner like my friend Valerie in the photo below.)

Why would you want to make a 1-hour quilt top?

Making 1-hour quilts is fun! It's really satisfying to just "get in and get done."

One-hour quilts let you make lots of quilts — fast — for lots of family, friends, or people in need.

One-hour quilts are meant to be used. You can make quilts for family and friends that they can enjoy. They won't put a quilt away in a closet and not use it because it's too precious. Or worse, they won't use a quilt you spent hundreds of hours (and dollars) making to lay on while they're working under the car. (ARGHGHGHGH!!!) You and they can feel good knowing that a 1-hour quilt is being used and loved, and if it gets worn out or ruined, you can easily replace it.

They are easy to quilt. You can quilt them on a domestic machine, without even marking them. And you don't need to do free-motion quilting — you can use a regular foot or a walking foot.

One-hour quilts let you coordinate decor. You can make a bunch of quilts and each one is different but they all coordinate. Make quilts for siblings who share a room, or maybe a bunk room in a beach house or cabin.

And along the lines of making lots of quilts fast, 1-hour quilts are great for making charity or disaster-relief quilts. Imagine getting a guild or a group of friends together and making a dozen or so quilts in an afternoon. These are so easy, even non-quilter friends can help.

I hope 1-hour quilts open up a whole new world of quilt-making enjoyment for you!

These are my friend Valerie's first two quilts ever! She made the strip set in one afternoon, then cut and sewed the two tops in two hours the next afternoon. (Luna supervised — woof!) You can see her next two 1-hour quilt tops on page 15.

That's What I'm Talkin' About! (Terms to know)

Before I go any further, let me define some terms so you'll know what I'm talking about. Some of these may already be familiar to you; others I had to invent specifically for 1-hour quilts. Note the abbreviations I've used as well. I'll use these throughout the book, especially in calculations and charts.

Rectangle Box Quilt: A rectangular quilt made by cutting the mother strip into a combination of trapezoids and triangles. (Illustration on page 6, pattern on page 35.)

Square Box Quilt: A square quilt made from cutting the mother strip into only triangles. (Illustration on page 6, pattern on page 49.)

Diamond-in-the-Square Quilt (DITS): A square quilt made of triangles set diagonally to create a diamond. (Illustration on page 6, pattern on page 57.)

Stripe Quilt: If you're using a whole-cloth border print, this is a quilt top made from the strip of fabric removed from one edge. It can be used as a top or as a backing for another quilt. (Illustration on page 6, pattern on page 63.)

Whole-Cloth Border Prints: Fabric printed with a border or large stripe pattern, usually (but not always) running length of fabric. For the purposes of this book, they can also be full-width gradations or any large design with a linear structure. You can find an in-depth discussion of border prints beginning on page 11.

Length of Fabric (LOF): Along the length of the fabric. When you buy fabric it is measured in length of fabric. Fabric can be measured or cut length of fabric. Designs are repeated length of fabric (see page 12).

Width of Fabric (WOF): Across the fabric from selvage to selvage. Fabric can be measured or cut width of fabric. A design can be repeated width of fabric (see page 13).

Mother Strip Terms
(You can learn about preparing mother strips on page 32. Each pattern will also have information about the mother strip specific to that pattern.)

Mother Strip: The entire strip of fabric — either whole cloth or strip set — before it is cut into triangles and trapezoids to make quilts. It will be several yards long before cutting.

Mother Strip Width (MSW): The width of the mother strip.

Mother Strip Length (MSL): The full length of the mother strip, before being cut down into quarter sections, trapezoids and/or triangles.

Quarter Section: When the mother strip is divided into four pieces for a Rectangular Box Quilt, each piece is a quarter section.

Standard Pattern: For each type of quilt listed, the pattern in this book gives it in a standard size, finishing to 58" wide. Each pattern includes a chart for adjusting it to make any size quilt.

Strip Set Terms
(You can learn more about strip sets on pages 19-23 and 69-79. Each pattern will also have information about building a strip set specific to that pattern.)

Strip Set: A mother strip built from a combination of component strips. Strip sets can be symmetrical or asymmetrical.

Asymmetrical Strip Set: A strip set with different fabrics across its width. It can have any number of component strips.

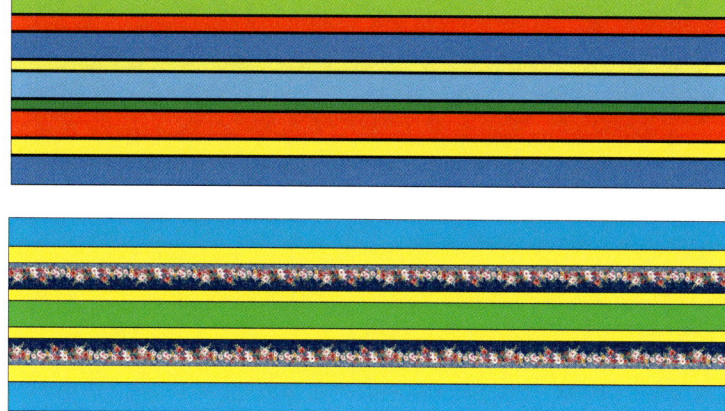

Symmetrical Strip Set: A strip set with the same order of fabrics right to left or left to right. It must have an uneven number of component strips.

Component Strip: A single strip of fabric that is a part of a strip set.

Component Strip Piece: A piece of fabric before it is sewn end-to-end with other pieces of the same fabric to make a component strip.

Rectangle Quilt Terms

Height of the Quilt (H): The finished measurement of the long sides of a rectangular quilt.

Width of the Quilt (W): The finished measurement of the short sides of a rectangular quilt.

Trapezoid: The shape that results when you cut triangles off the ends of a quarter section. In a Rectangle Box quilt, the long sides of the quilt are made from trapezoids.

End Triangle: The triangles that form the short sides of a Rectangle Box quilt.

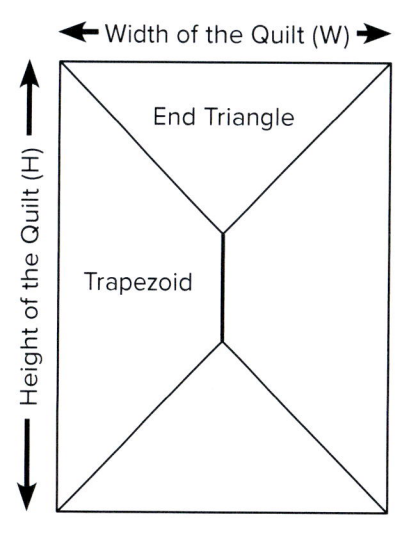

Square Quilt Terms

Height-Width (HW): The finished measurement of the sides of a Square Box or Diamond-in-the-Square quilt; height and width are equal so they are treated as the same unit for calculation purposes.

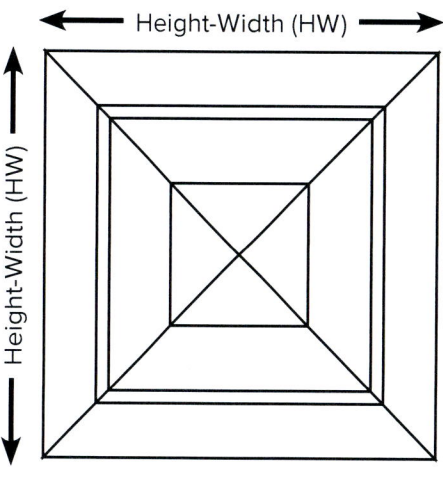

TERMS TO KNOW

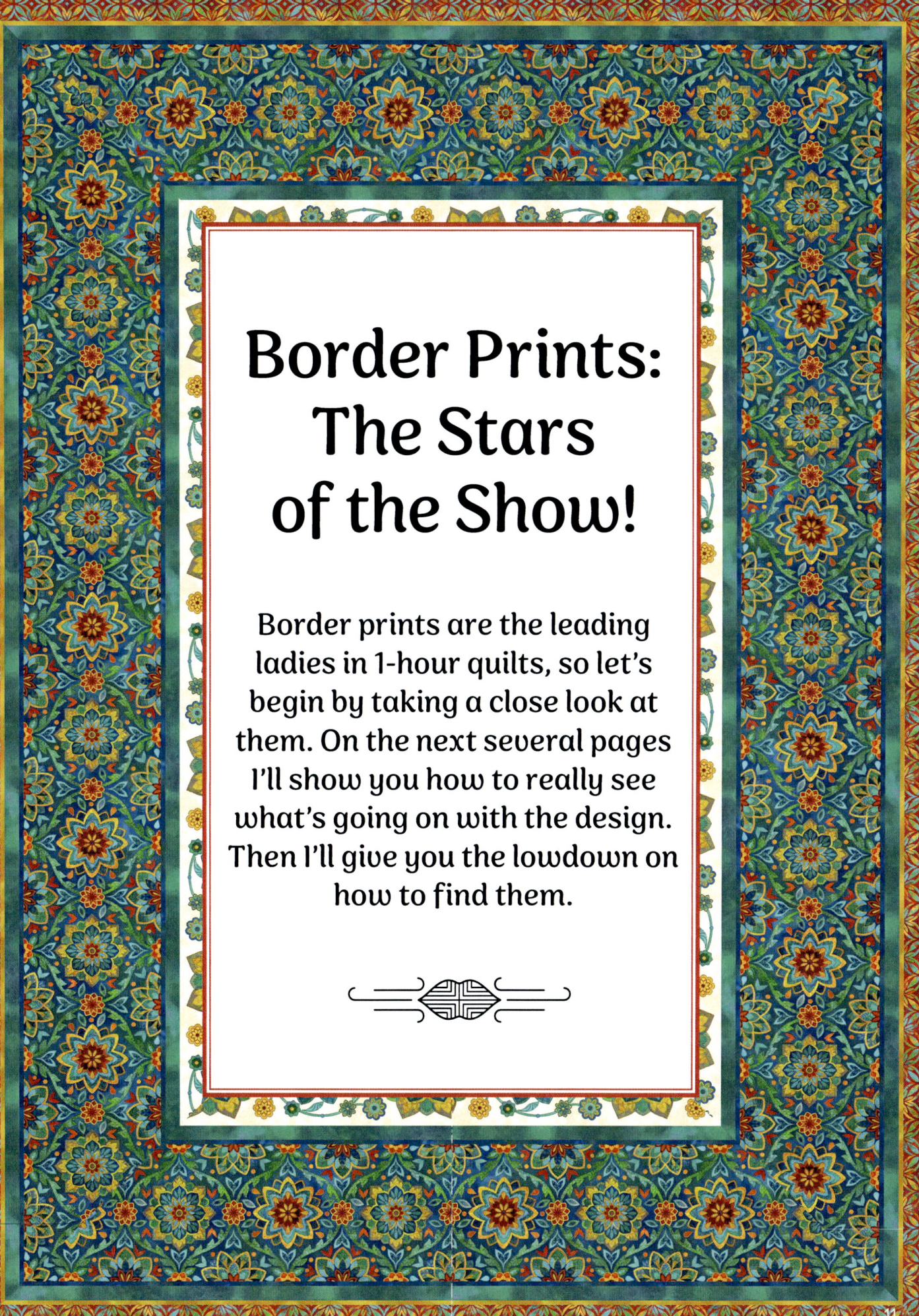

Border Prints: The Stars of the Show!

Border prints are the leading ladies in 1-hour quilts, so let's begin by taking a close look at them. On the next several pages I'll show you how to really see what's going on with the design. Then I'll give you the lowdown on how to find them.

Looking at Border Prints

When you begin to look closely at border prints, you'll discover there are a surprising number of variations in design, repeats and symmetry. For our purposes here, border prints include large stripes, some gradations and any fabric with a large linear structure. The best border prints for 1-hour quilts have a variety of different stripes in the design — the more variety, the more interesting the quilt. You can use border prints whole, or mix them with other fabrics in a strip set.

As you become more aware of the structure of the designs in border prints you may discover similar design features in "regular" fabrics as well. These could be useful for building a strip set, or might even carry over into your other quilts as well.

Each pattern will tell you how much whole-cloth border print is needed to make the standard pattern size. It also has a table showing measurements and yardages needed to adjust the pattern for any size quilt.

Repeats

Length of Fabric (LOF) Repeats

All quilting fabrics repeat their designs along the length of the fabric. The repeat usually occurs every 24" or in divisions of 24" such as 12", 8", 6", 4", etc. (Digital printing is starting to change this.) Depending on the design of the fabric, the repeat may or may not impact the design of your quilts.

With softer designs that blend together like the example at right, there's no need to think about matching a repeat where seams join at corners or in the middle of an end triangle. The pattern will blend no matter where the repeats happen to fall.

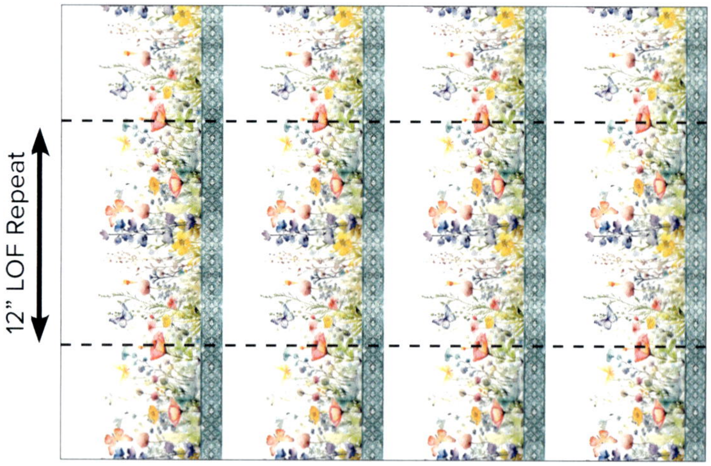

Butterfly Fantasy by Jason Yenter for In the Beginning Fabrics

But if the design has a very strong structure like this example, you might want to size the quilt height and mother strip length to fit the repeat. For example, if the repeat is 12", you would make the height of the quilt a multiple of 12, such as 84" or 96". Then base the length of the mother strip on that length.

If you want to match LOF repeats, buy extra fabric and count repeats when you're measuring fabric.

Read more about cutting repeats on page 29.

Farm-tastic Friends by Sweet Cee Creative for Studio E

Width of Fabric (WOF) Repeats

Border prints and large stripes usually repeat a design across the width of fabric. The width of the repeat varies depending on how many copies of the design fit from selvage to selvage.

A border print with multiple repeats of the same design across width of fabric won't make a very interesting quilt by itself (see the *Glorious Garden* mock-ups on page 17). But, cutting apart the repeats and joining them for a component strip within a strip set is a great way to get the design strength of a large print within a variety of fabrics. It's a also a great way to use a border fabric if you don't have a lot of it. Take a look at *Blue Daisies* on page 48 to see how the daisy fabric became the focal point of that quilt.

Dragon Friends by Jason Yenter for In the Beginning Fabrics

Full Width of Fabric Design

Full-width fabrics are have a single design from selvage to selvage. Gradations can also fall into this category. They still have LOF repeats, but do not have WOF repeats. The examples at right (and *Wild Blossoms* page 17) are all full-width design fabrics. These fabrics are uncommon, but when you find them they make glorious 1-hour quilts.

If you reduce the width of a full-width design fabric to make your mother strip, consider carefully which side of the yardage you're willing to lose. Fold and photograph the fabric with each side missing to get a sense of how the resulting quilts will look. Compare the mock-ups of *Boho Blooms* on page 16 to see how different the quilts can be: the first set has the red side cut off and second set has the green side cut off. Another option might be to cut out a section of the middle and sew the two outside sections together.

Boho Blooms by Deborah Edwards for Northcott Fabrics

Bee Haven by Rachel Rossi for Benartex

LOOKING AT BORDER PRINTS

Symmetry & Asymmetry

Symmetrical Stripes

A symmetrical stripe is a mirror image (or very close it) within itself. You can fold it in half and it will look identical or pretty much the same on both sides. Symmetrical stripes often have symmetrical separating lines between them as well. The sunflower fabric at right is an example of a symmetrical stripe in a WOF repeat. Even though the stripes aren't exact mirror images within the stripe, the flowers are a soft enough design that they could blend together and give the feeling of being symmetrical.

Sunflower Farm by Chong A Hwang for Timeless Treasures

Asymmetrical Stripes

An asymmetrical stripe is different from side to within itself. Pay attention to the direction that you cut and sew these if you use them in a strip set, so they all face the same direction. The blue floral at right is an example of an asymmetrical stripe in four WOF repeats (see mock-ups on page 17).

Glorious Garden by Kathleen Winslow Gardner for In the Beginning Fabrics

Varied Stripes

Sometimes a fabric will have a variety of different stripes across the width of fabric. In some cases, several stripes are repeated (like the sunflower fabric above). In others, each stripe is different (these could be considered a form of full-width design). The tea-party themed fabric at right is an excellent example of a border fabric with all different stripes (see mock-ups on page 16).

Let's Bake by Ronnie Thomas for Studio E

The quilt on the cover was made from an unusual African fabric that had all different stripes across the width of the fabric. The hand-drawn designs and bold colors created quite a lively and colorful quilt!

Symmetry in Both Directions

Sometimes a large, structured fabric can be cut in stripes even though it's not a border print. Often these are symmetrical, sometimes in both directions like the examples at right. Experiment with these fabrics in different directions — you may discover that they behave in surprising ways!

African fabric, unknown designer / manufacturer

True Colors by Danielle Duer for Benartex

Be Careful with These Border Prints

Some border prints have design along the selvages, and a lot of empty space in the middle. In two quilts made from the same mother strip, one quilt will have a strong border around the outside, while the other one will have a busy center and a plain outer edge. You can see the difference in this pair of rectangle box quilts below, made by my friend Valerie. I helped her pick out this fabric — and learned from it!

This type of border print is best used in a strip set, so that other fabrics can provide some needed interest and contrast. In retrospect, I would have cut this fabric differently, to use only the patterned part and save the plainer parts for backing.

Green border fabric: *Desert Oasis, Wind Whips*, Create Joy Project for Moda
Peach fabric: *Serenity* by Clothworks
Turquoise fabric: *Stripes Collection* by Riley Blake Designs

Which brings us to strip sets . . .

If you can't find a border print, or you want to use a border print for only part of your quilt, or you don't want to use a border print at all, build a strip set. We'll explore strip sets beginning on page 19.

LOOKING AT BORDER PRINTS   15

Comparing Border Prints

Look at these examples to see how structures of border print fabrics will look made up into box and stripe quilts.

Boho Blooms
by Deborah Edwards for Northcott
This full-width design features stripes of different widths, colors and values. The box quilts that result from it resemble Oriental rugs. Each is quite different depending on which portion of the fabric is used.

Let's Bake
by Ronnie Thomas for Studio E
A variety of different patterns in different stripes

Red edge cut off   Green edge cut off

Box Quilt 1

Box Quilt 1
(center image below Boho Blooms, green edge cut off)

Box Quilt 1

Box Quilt 2

Box Quilt 2

Box Quilt 2

Stripe Quilt

Stripe Quilt
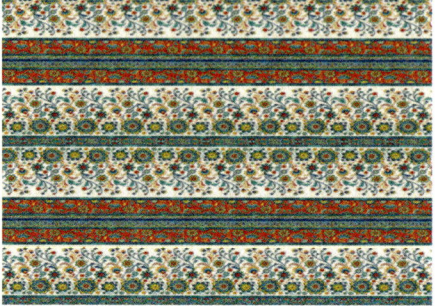

Stripe Quilt

16   THE 1-HOUR QUILT TOP

Wild Blossoms
by Robin Pickens for Moda
A single continuous gradation of flowers from one color to another

Glorious Garden
by Kathleen Winslow Gardner
for In the Beginning
Four repeats of the same asymmetrical stripe

Box Quilt 1

Box Quilt 1

Box Quilt 2

Box Quilt 2

Stripe Quilt

Stripe Quilt

COMPARING BORDER PRINTS

How to Find Border Print Fabrics

▶ Check your local quilt shop. It's not unusual to find border prints on the bargain shelf, so check there first!

▶ Go to the website of any fabric manufacturer and type the word "border" into the Search window. This will bring up fabrics in their collection that have the word Border in the title or description. However, fabrics don't always have Border in the title or description, so dig a little deeper: go through the catalog and click on the names of the collections. Within the collection you'll often find a border print.

▶ Sometimes fabrics are on the manufacturer's website but aren't yet in stores. In this case, you'll see a note that says something like "Shipping [Month] [Year]" on the collection. You'll have to wait until it ships — if you love it it's worth the wait!

▶ Once you've found a fabric you like, check your local quilt shop first to see if they have it. If not, search online for the manufacturer and collection name to find stores online that sell that fabric.

▶ Do an online search for "Border Print Fabrics" and see what pops up. Use the results to start your search with fabric manufacturers or fabric stores.

> Keep in mind that the fabrics shown in this book were only available at the time of writing. Fabric companies typically produce a fabric line for six months to a year, then discontinue it to bring out newer designs. Use the search techniques above to research currently-available fabrics.

Auditioning Border Print Fabrics

If you find a fabric online and want to see how it will play out in a quilt, use a graphic design program such as Photoshop or Illustrator to do a mock-up like the ones on pages 16-17. Usually you can save the online image of the fabric by right-clicking on the image and selecting "Save image as". Save it (JPG or PNG format) then open the image in your design program and copy, cut, and rotate pieces to create mock-up quilt designs.

If you're not comfortable working in a graphic design program, print copies of the image on paper, then cut and paste them together.

If you're in a fabric shop (lucky you!) and want to audition a border print fabric, fold it to create a mitered corner to get a better sense of how it will look in a box quilt. 1. Unroll a length of fabric from the bolt. 2. Fold the loose end back over the bolt end. 3. Open the loose end diagonally to create a mitered corner. If the fabric has a repeat, try to center the fold on the repeat for the best preview.

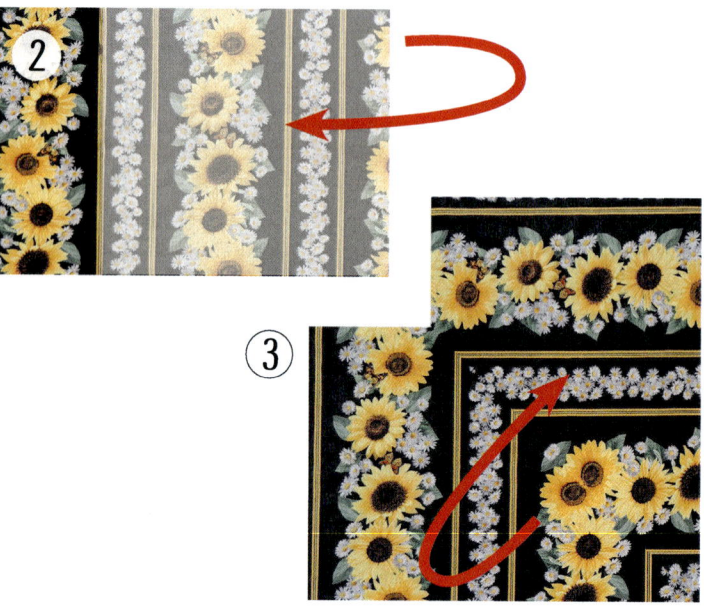

18   THE 1-HOUR QUILT TOP

Strip Sets: The Supporting Cast

If you can't find a border print you like, or you just want to be more creative with your fabric choices, build a strip set. Tools for building strip sets begin on page 69.

Looking at Strip Sets

Any 1-hour quilt can be made with a strip set. Using a strip set for the mother strip gives you the creative freedom to choose your own combination of fabrics: mix fabrics around a border print fabric, or skip using a border print altogether.

Building a strip set will add time to your 1-hour quilts — how much depends on how many component strips you include in the set. However, once you get the strip set made, making the quilt tops will still take about an hour per top.

In the standard patterns, using a strip set for the mother strip will give you two Rectangle Box or Square Box quilts, or one Diamond-in-the-Square quilt. It won't make the Stripe quilt because you don't have the excess fabric strip that is left over from reducing the width of fabric from 44" to the mother strip width. Each pattern will also tell you how to adjust for a single quilt.

As you read through the pages that follow, look at the quilts on pages 75-79. The strips sets and planning charts are shown with the quilts, so you can see how each strip set was built and how it looked in the finished quilt. Learn from these examples as you build your own strip sets and make them into quilts.

Strip Set Structure

Strip sets can be symmetrical or asymmetrical.
Use component strips of different widths for variety.

Asymmetrical Strip Set

Asymmetrical Strip Set

▶ Has different fabrics across the width of the strip

▶ Most commonly used for making any 1-hour quilt

Symmetrical Strip Set

▶ Has the same order of fabrics from left to right or right to left

▶ Must have an odd number of strips so that the center strip is in the same position from either left or right

▶ If you use a border print with an asymmetrical stripe, place the stripes in mirror position to each other

Symmetrical Strip Set
Same in both directions

Use a symmetrical strip set when:

- You're making a single Rectangle Box or Square Box quilt
- You want two sister quilts to be the same

20   THE 1-HOUR QUILT TOP

Choosing Fabrics for a Strip Set

Creating a beautiful quilt from a strip set begins with a strong combination of fabrics. Here's what to look for:

Use a mix of four types of fabric, plus different values

1. Large prints (often border print fabric) to give focus and personality. Also, the colors in this fabric will dictate the colors in the other fabrics.

2. Small multicolor prints bring energy and detail. Sometimes these can be geometrics.

3. Geometric designs (stripes, plaids, diamonds, etc.) create rhythm, provide contrast to softer textures and build structure. Sometimes these are a stripe within a border print.

4. Solids or monochrome textures contain busy designs and provide structure.

Finally, make sure there is a mix of light, medium and dark values among your fabrics.

A large print fabric. This was not a border print but the figures were arranged in symmetrical rows.

Because this stripe had so much color, it worked as both a small multicolor print and a geometric.

I fussy-cut the stripe to get the red/gold and green in longer strips. Triangles add detail and scale to the mix.

This solid green helps hold structure between all those busy prints

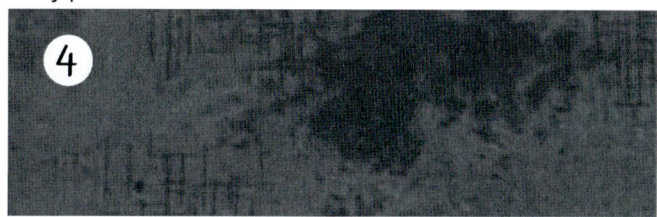

The mix of fabrics in the strip set

The Rectangle Box Quilts made from the strip set

CHOOSING FABRICS FOR A STRIP SET

Placing Fabrics Within a Strip Set

Study the examples on pages 75-79 as you explore the concepts here.

Begin with the key fabric — usually this will be the border print or large print fabric. Use this fabric as a guide to pull coordinating colors.

Besides using the key fabric to choose colors, pay attention to its *proportion* of colors: for example, there might a lot of blue and just a little red. You might find that keeping this proportion of colors in the strip set creates a pleasing combination. On the other hand, you might decide to punch up a color that appears only in small amounts. It's your choice — just make it a choice, not an accident.

Alternate strips of light and dark fabrics for contrast and structure.

Separate soft designs (like florals) with solids or geometric designs (like stripes) for clear structure.

Place similar values and/or textures next to each other ONLY if you want to blend the design.

Try using two shades of the same color to create variety without making the strip set feel too busy.

If you use the same fabric multiple times, try different widths in different places for variety, unless you're using it as a consistent spacer (like I did in the Blue Daisy quilts).

If you have a really strong fabric, either use just a little bit so it doesn't take over, or make it the focus.

A single component strip can have different fabrics, but the value (light/medium/dark) should be the same within that strip. However, there can be exceptions, as you can see in this vintage kantha quilt from India.

In Carolina's quilt, the turquoise and black rings contain different fabrics, but you don't notice because the color and value match.

In this vintage kantha quilt, notice how the fabrics in some rings don't all match. The different colors are a dynamic surprise in the composition!
(Photo courtesy of quilter/designer Amy Butler.)

In box quilts, the outer fabrics of the strip set create the centers and borders of the two sister quilts. Use different fabrics in these strips to make the sister quilts unique. Outer strips should be at least 4" wide to have some weight and presence. They should not be less than 2" because you'll lose about 1" of design to seam allowances in the center of each quilt.

If a fabric has a structured design, try to fussy-cut the component strip pieces so that the design lines up along the strip. You may need to buy extra fabric to allow for this.

Sometimes an easier way to work with stripes is to cut across the stripe, eliminating the need to line them up.

Always ask yourself "What if?" and try it. Try doing the exact opposite of what you think might work. Don't be afraid to try something unexpected that breaks the rules. Whether you like the outcome or not, you'll learn something from it. And if you love it, go with it!

Building Your Strip Set

Experiment first. Lay fabrics side-by-side and play with different combinations, different widths, different neighbors. As you audition possibilities, take lots of pictures. Try using a black & white filter on a photo to check contrast and structure, independent of color.

Using a strip set in the standard patterns

▶ Make a copy of the Strip Set Planning Chart on page 71. Use it to plan your strip set, including both finished and cut sizes for each component strip.

▶ Each pattern has a Strip Set Yardage Chart. Use it to find the yardage needed for each component strip. Fill in the yardages on the Strip Set Planning Chart.

▶ Using a strip set for quilts in other sizes:

▶ Use the Changing Size Chart in the standard pattern to determine length and width of the mother strip.

▶ Use the Strip Set Planning Chart to plan your strip set.

▶ Use the Component Strip Yardage Chart on page 73 to find the yardage needed for each component strip and fill it in on the Strip Set Planning Chart.

BUILDING A STRIP SET   23

The Patterns

Following are four patterns for 1-hour quilts: Rectangle Box, Square Box, Diamond-in-the-Square and Stripe.

Each pattern is given in a standard size, based on a finished width of 58".

Also included are instructions for adjusting to any size you wish.

THE STANDARD PATTERNS

About the Standard Patterns

All 1-hour quilts begin with a "mother strip"— a long strip of whole-cloth border print fabric or a strip set. The mother strip gets cut into various sections, then the sections are recombined to make the quilts.

To keep things simple, I've created standard patterns for all four quilts, sized to 58" wide. The Rectangle Box and Stripe quilts are 58" x 80"; the Square Box and Diamond-in-the-Square (DITS) quilts are 58" x 58".

Because of how the mother strip is configured and cut, each pattern makes two "sister" quilts. If you make them from a whole-cloth border print, the mother strip may also make a stripe quilt.

Why 58" x 80"?

▶ It's a great size for a couch or cuddle quilt.

▶ It fits on top of a queen or double size bed, so it can add warmth and style over another quilt or comforter without the extra bulk, weight and cost of a larger quilt.

▶ Since a twin bed is 39" wide by 75" long, the 58" width lets it hang over the sides and the 80" height is just enough to hang over the foot of the bed while covering the shoulders of the person sleeping in it.

▶ It fits on Minkee™. Minkee is super-cuddly as a backing so it's great for quilts that are going to be used and loved. It comes 60" or 90" wide, so if you use it to back a quilt 58" x 80" there's no need to piece the backing. (This was my longarm quilter's suggestion - thank you Mary!)

What if I want to make a different size quilt?

No problem! Making a 1-hour quilt is more about the process than a particular pattern. So, you can use the process to make any size quilt, from baby to king size. Each pattern includes a Changing Size Chart to help you adjust to other sizes and figure the yardage you'll need to make them.

Can I make just one quilt?

Yes, *IF* you use a symmetrical mother strip. Each pattern includes adjustments for making a single quilt.

Box Quilt 1

Box Quilt 2

Stripe Quilt

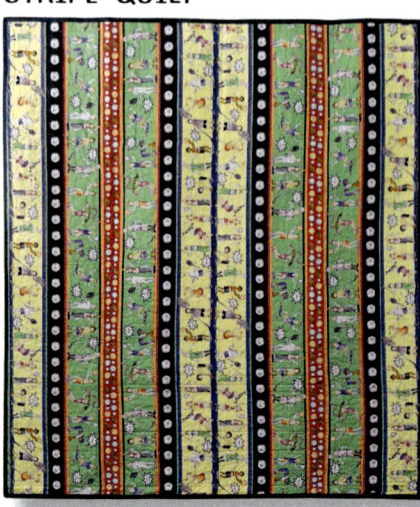

If you're working with a whole-cloth border print fabric to make Rectangle Box or Square Box quilts, the standard pattern will give you three quilts: two box quilts and one stripe quilt. You can use the stripe quilt as a backing for one of the other quilts, if you wish.

Tools

You'll need these basic sewing tools

▶ Standard sewing tools (scissors, pins, etc.)

▶ Rotary cutter & mat (start with a fresh, sharp blade, as you will be cutting through multiple layers of fabric at seams)

▶ 3-5 rotary cutting rulers, one square, the others long (see below)

▶ Painter's tape for stabilizing bias-cut edges, labeling fabrics, joining and marking rulers, etc.

▶ Iron & ironing board or tabletop ironing mat

▶ Sewing machine

▶ Regular sewing foot for assembly (can be 1/4" foot but doesn't have to be)

▶ Walking foot for quilting (optional, but really helpful)

▶ Free-motion foot for quilting (optional)

▶ Water-soluble, non-toxic glue such as Elmer's School Glue (used for binding)

Why do I need so many rulers?

Since you'll be cutting some really big triangles, it will help to have a really big ruler, especially one with an accurate 90-degree angle. If you're like me, you have several rotary cutting rulers of various sizes around your studio. Just tape them together to make a big V! It was too big to show in the photo, but I actually taped one more ruler to the end of one of the long rulers shown here, so that my giant ruler would reach all the way across a 29-1/2" mother strip for a full-width cut.

Batting

I am a huge fan of fusible batting, and Hobbs Heirloom Premium Fusible 80/20 is my favorite. It's double-sided, repositionable, and lets go after the quilting is done, so the quilt is soft. Two Queen size rolls will make three quilts 58" x 80".

Heirloom Premium Fusible 80/20 made in the USA by Hobbs Bonded Fibers. See page 81 for sources.

When you need to piece fusible batting together there's no need to sew it: just smash the pieces up tight against each other and iron. A couple of pins at the edges will help keep everything stable until the layers are quilted.

Ask for it at your local quilt shop — if they don't have it, ask them to order it. If you order it online try Hancock's of Paducah or Connecting Threads.

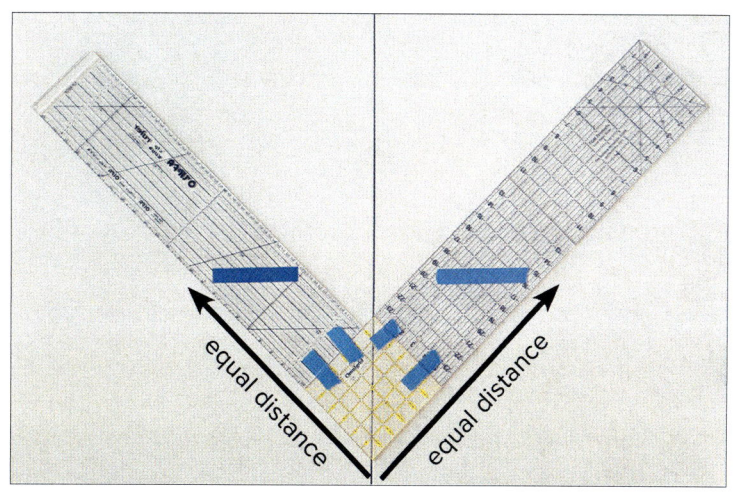

To make sure the V doesn't tip to one side or the other, measure from the V-tip to a reference point in the mother strip — a seam or a line in the design — along one arm of the V. Then, measure that distance up the other arm (don't rely on the ruler markings, because the rulers will probably be different). Mark both points with tape or a marker. (Sharpie will not rub off but can be erased with alcohol when you're ready.) When using the ruler, align the marks on both arms to the same line on the mother strip so the diagonal cuts and angles will be accurate.

Techniques

On the next few pages you'll find some techniques that I've found particularly useful in making 1-hour quilts. They are presented in the order you would use them: cutting, pinning, sewing. In addition, instructions for sewing Y-seams can be found on pages 44-47.

Tearing vs. Cutting Fabric

I love to "Snip, Grip and Rip." Tearing fabric is fast, easy, and — most importantly — always straight on grain. You can tear width of fabric or length of fabric. You can rip strips of almost any width. I rip fabric even for binding strips 2-1/2" to 3" wide.

That said, the narrower a strip is, the better it is to cut rather than tear. I typically cut strips narrower than 2".

Of course, if you need to be really accurate, cutting is the better choice. And cutting is essential for diagonal cuts.

To tear, nick the fabric with a cut about 1" into the fabric. You can nick at the edge and rip all the way across or nick on a fold and tear from the middle to the edges. Since you'll lose a few threads on either side of the ripped strip, make the nick about 1/8" wider than the finished strip size you want. Now pull hard and rip!

On width-of-fabric tears, usually you can rip right through the selvage. But, sometimes the selvage has a really strong thread in it that doesn't break easily. If that happens, snip through the selvage to separate the strips. Or, cut off the selvage before you begin.

Valerie and I tearing fabric. (I'm behind the camera.)

Be aware: If fabric has previously been cut in the direction you're going to tear, even though the cut edge looks straight it might not be on-grain. If you tear along that edge the torn strip might be tapered, leaving one end too narrow. So, make your first tear far enough from the cut edge that it leaves room to square the fabric to the grain.

After tearing, iron the strip to flatten the edges, as they will roll a bit. As for the straggling threads, I simply remove them as I go through the construction process if they get in the way.

Tearing fabric takes just a few seconds per cut — even (or especially) for really big pieces of fabric. Since these quilts are all about working fast, tearing will save you lots of time. Do it with a friend and have fun together. Or, do it when you've had a bad day and enjoy letting your frustration go!

When to tear vs. cut

Whole-cloth fabric: Tear lengthwise to reduce 44" fabric to the size of your mother strip. Then, tear across the mother strip to make the four quarter-sections of a Rectangle Box quilt.

Strip sets: Tear all the component strip pieces, then sew them together end-to-end. After constructing a strip set for a mother strip, you must CUT across it since you'll be cutting across seams.

Diagonal (Bias) cuts: All diagonal cuts MUST be cut, not torn.

Cutting Repeats

If your fabric has a design with a strong structure, getting repeats to look good in your quilt begins with cutting the mother strip correctly. If you are buying a fabric with obvious repeats — particularly if they are symmetrical — get extra yardage for matching repeats.

You may want to adjust the length of the mother strip so that you can cut it into sections at the same point in the repeat. This will ensure that the repeats match across the width of the quilt and the corners will all look pretty much the same.

Example 1A: This section was NOT cut with the repeats centered. See how the ends of the section are different? When the quilt is assembled, the repeats don't align across the width (yellow arrow) and the corners are different.

Example 1B: This section was cut with matching repeats on each end so the design is centered. Here, when the quilt is assembled, the repeats align across the width (yellow arrow) and the corners are all the same.

Example 2: Let's say your fabric has a 12" LOF repeat and you're making the Rectangle Box quilt. Make the mother strip long enough to cut the quarter sections 84" long (instead of 81" long, the length in the standard pattern), because 84 is a multiple of 12. When you cut the quarter sections, place the cuts at the same position in the repeat and you have a better chance of the corners all looking the same. Keep in mind, however, that the design may not match perfectly at the corners because the seam is diagonal, not square.

About 1/4" Seam Allowances

All of the quilt measurements and sizing in this book are based on 1/4" seam allowances. But don't stress: these quilts don't require absolute precision, so if your seams are a little less or a little more than 1/4", the quilt should still go together just fine. Ease pieces to fit if necessary (no one will ever know or care).

Folding & Cutting Accurate Diagonals

1. Square up mother strips

Square off ends of the mother strip and quarter sections. Align fabric to the cutting mat grid; then align the ruler to lines and seams in the mother strip and the cutting mat grid.

2. Make accurate diagonal folds

Fold the end of the strip diagonally to the edge. Face right sides together so seam allowances don't warp the fold. Pin along outer edge and fold. Place pins about 2" back so scissors can fit into the fold.

3. Make accurate diagonal cuts

Insert scissors into the fold and pull outward so the tension places the cut exactly at the fold. You could also use a rotary cutter and ruler; take care that the ruler doesn't slip and cut too far into the fold.

4. Trim pieces to the same size

After cutting triangles off the mother strip, stack the matching triangles and trapezoids for each quilt and check that they are the same size. Trim down larger ones if necessary.

Pinning to Match Lines & Points

How you pin makes a huge difference in helping lines and points match. Use this two-pin method that I call "acupuncture pinning" to keep them aligned while sewing.

1. Working from the side you will sew from, stick a pin precisely through any points you want to match.

2. Pinch the fabric together on the shaft of the pin.

3. Stick a second pin diagonally and almost flat through all the pinned layers, entering the fabric precisely at the base of the first pin. Bring it back up through the fabric as far from the entry point as possible. The first pin prevents the layers from shifting. Remove the first pin. When you sew, carefully put the needle down precisely at the entry point of the second pin (remove it just before you take the stitch) and the points will match.

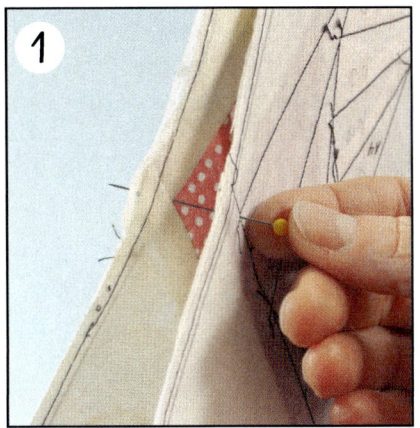 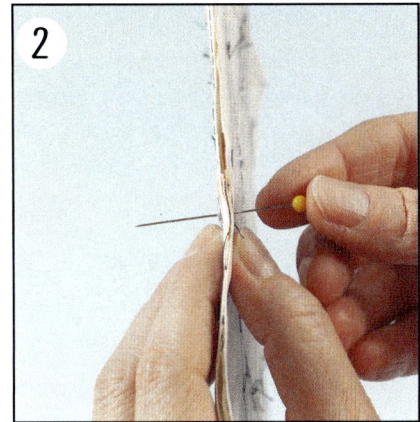 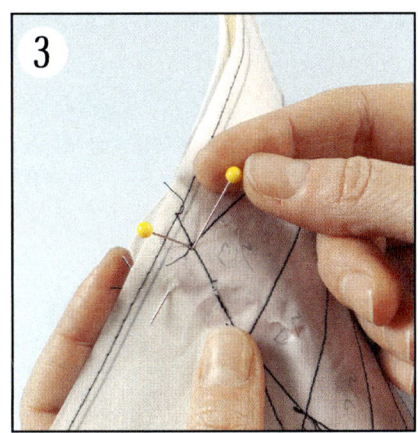

Interlocking Seams to Match Corners

Getting your corners to match is easy with this simple "interlock" technique.

A. Press seams in opposite directions. When you position the seams face-to-face to sew them together, the ridges of the seams face in opposite directions so they will lock together.

B. When sewing, place on top the layer that has seam allowances facing away from you. The forward pressure of the top layer moving through the foot will push the top ridge toward the bottom ridge, locking them against each other, and your corners will be tight and clean.

C. "Pinwheel" the seams where corners meet. Open the seams where they intersect so that each seam allowance faces in a different direction. This distributes the bulk, so you don't get a lump at the point.

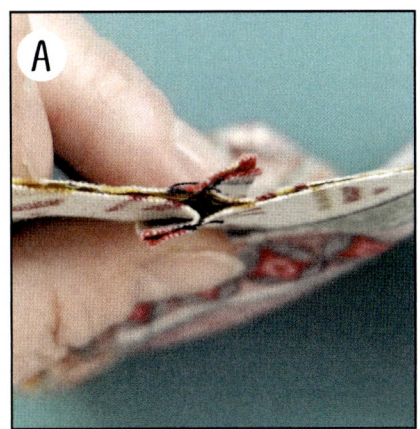 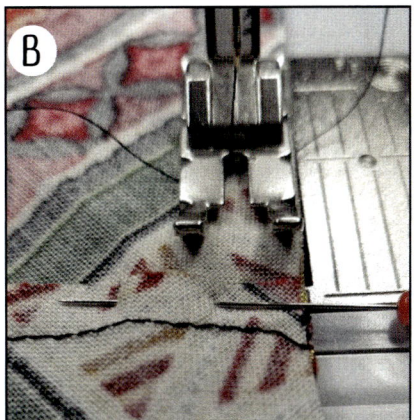 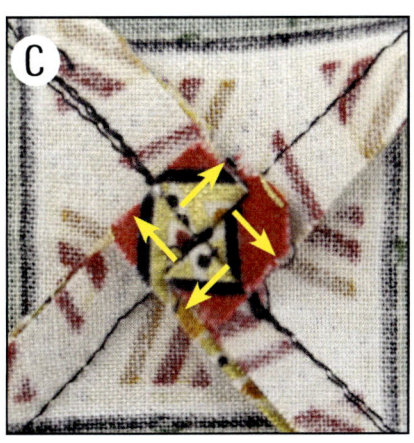

TECHNIQUES: PINNING & INTERLOCKING SEAMS

Preparing the Mother Strip

The first step in any 1-hour quilt is preparing the mother strip from which all the pieces will be cut. The mother strip can be either a whole-cloth border print or a strip set made from several component strips.

For Whole-Cloth Mother Strips

Since quilting fabric is 44" wide, you'll need to reduce the width of the fabric to the width of the mother strip. Each pattern will tell you the width needed. (Usually it's 29-1/2". If you're making a different size, check the Changing Size table in the pattern.) Remove a strip of fabric along one selvage to bring the width down to the required size.

Before you remove this strip, audition the fabric and decide which selvage you want to keep. (Look at the *Boho Blooms* examples on page 16 to see how different the quilts can look depending on which edge you remove.) The selvage you keep will be outside edge of one of the box quilts or the largest part of a diamond quilt. Remove the width along the OTHER selvage.

In all diagrams throughout the book, the mother strip is green and the removed strip is blue.

Measure the width of the mother strip across one end of the fabric, starting from the selvage you are keeping (red arrow at right). Snip at this point. Now tear all the way to the other end.

(Yes, I said tear. Really. It's the fastest, most accurate way to do this. If you need reassurance, read page 28.)

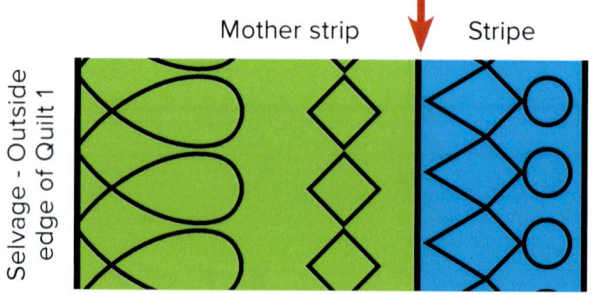

Set aside the removed strip for a Stripe quilt or to use as backing. In the case of the Diamond-in-the-Square quilt, in the standard pattern both strips are equal, so each strip can make one DITS quilt.

For Strip Set Mother Strips

Each pattern gives you the mother strip length (MSL) and mother strip width (MSW). Use the Strip Set Planning Chart on 71 to build your strip set to these dimensions. There is no removed strip (so no third quilt).

You'll need to know how much yardage is required for each component strip. The Strip Set Yardage Chart in each pattern will give you the amount of fabric needed for any width of strip, based on that Standard Pattern.

For Different Sizes

Each pattern includes a Changing Sizes Chart for adjusting the dimensions of the quilt to any size you want. Find your desired quilt size in the chart, and it will tell you the mother strip length, the mother strip width and the yardage needed. Then, begin by either reducing your whole-cloth border fabric, or building your strip set, to that size.

Can I make two quilts of different sizes?

Yes and no.

Rectangle Box quilts: Because both quilts are cut from the same mother strip, both quilts must be the same WIDTH, but you can make two quilts of different HEIGHTS. It's easiest with Half & Half construction: instead of dividing the mother strip into four equal quarter sections, cut two quarter sections longer and two shorter. Just keep in mind all quarter sections must be longer than twice the mother strip width. If you want to plan ahead, add together two heights of the longer size and two heights of the shorter size to figure the length of the mother strip.

Square Box quilts: Because the proportions of the right isosceles triangles that build these quilts cannot change, both quilts that come from one mother strip are naturally the same size. You could cut the triangles smaller after they are cut from the mother strip to get a smaller quilt, if you wanted to do that.

Diamond-in-the-Square quilts: Since each quilt is made completely from one mother strip, the mother strips could be different widths, resulting in quilts of different sizes.

Can I make just one quilt?

Yes. A section on adjusting for a single quilt can be found in each pattern. For Rectangle Box and Square Box quilts, the mother strip MUST be symmetrical. For Diamond-in-the-Square quilts it can be asymmetrical.

For whole-cloth border print fabric: When you remove the excess width, cut at a position that keeps the design symmetrical across the width of the mother strip. If the border print you want to use is not symmetrical, build it into a symmetrical strip set.

For strip sets: Build a symmetrical strip set.

The strip set for the Garden Quilts

The African Quilts

These two quilts were the seeds of this book — the original Rectangle Box quilts. I found the fabric in an African store near my home in NYC. The quilts are whole-cloth: the hand-drawn stripes are printed onto the fabric, not pieced as a strip set.

I made this quilt for my niece to take to college.

I kept this quilt even though at the time I didn't know what I would do with it. Now it's a sample to take along for classes and trunk shows.

The third quilt that came from this fabric is the Stripe quilt on page 62. I used it as backing for this quilt.

34   THE 1-HOUR QUILT TOP

Rectangle Box Quilts

Rectangle Box quilts are built from triangles and trapezoids. The standard pattern here makes two quilts 58" x 80". For different sizes, use the table on page 37. If you want to make only one quilt, refer to the instructions on page 41.

Two Construction Methods

I'm giving you two methods for sewing Rectangle Box quilts: the **Half & Half** method and the **Y-Seam** method. Before beginning, you need to choose which method you're going to use, because the yardage for the mother strip is different with each one. If you're not sure, get enough fabric for the Y-seam method.

Half & Half construction (pages 38-42) is easiest. In this method you construct two rectangular halves then join them with a seam down the middle of the quilt. This method has the advantage of avoiding Y-seams, but requires that you carefully match lines or component strips in the middle of the end triangles. This method uses the whole mother strip, with no fabric left over.

Y-Seam construction (pages 44-47) requires Y-seams. Its advantage is that the lines in the fabric or the seams in a strip set are continuous across the end triangles of the quilt, which avoids breaking a very structured design. The Y-seam method is a bit more challenging, but before you start shaking in your boots about Y-seams, take a look at the instructions. They actually are not hard if you use a few simple techniques that ensure points match accurately. With the Y-seam method, the mother strip needs to be longer, because a small triangle at the each end of it goes unused.

Materials for the Standard Pattern

Whole-cloth fabric: This table gives the mother strip dimensions and yardage for the standard pattern. The yardage makes three quilts; the removed strip of fabric makes a Stripe quilt, page 63.

	HALF & HALF CONSTRUCTION	Y-SEAM CONSTRUCTION
MOTHER STRIP LENGTH (MSL):	324" (9 yards)	354" (round up to 360", 10 yards)
MOTHER STRIP WIDTH (MSW):	29-1/2"	

Note: These are minimums. Make the strip a bit longer if you want insurance.

Strip set: Follow fabric selection guidelines on pages 20-23. Build an asymmetrical strip set. This makes two quilts; there is no third quilt because you build the strip, rather than reduce the width of yardage.

▶ **Binding:** 2/3 yard for each 58" x 80" quilt. (Refer to the Binding Chart on page 66 for different sizes.)

▶ **Backing:** 2-1/3 yards of Minkee 60" wide for each quilt or 1-3/4 yards of Minkee 90" wide for each quilt
OR 3-1/2 yards quilting fabric 44" wide for each quilt
Refer to the Backing Yardage Chart on page 68 for different sizes.

▶ **Batting:** 2 Queen size rolls will make three quilts 58" x 80" (including a Stripe Quilt)
If you use Minkee for backing, batting is optional

▶ **Thread:** for assembly and for quilting

Rectangle Box Quilt: Standard Pattern Strip Set Yardage Chart

MSL = 324" (9 YDS)		IF CUTTING LOF			IF CUTTING WOF	
STRIP WIDTH		# OF LOF STRIPS YOU CAN CUT ACROSS WOF	YARDAGE NEEDED TO CUT LOF (INCHES & YDS)		# OF WOF STRIPS TO CUT	YARDAGE NEEDED TO CUT WOF (INCHES & YDS)
FINISHED STRIP WIDTH	CUT WIDTH		WOF = 42" (44" MINUS SELVAGES, INCLUDES SEAM ALLOWANCES FOR JOINING STRIP ENDS)			
21	21.5	2				172" / 4-7/8 yds
20.5	21	2				168" / 4-2/3 yds
20	20.5	2				164" / 4-5/8 yds
19.5	20	2				160" / 4-1/2 yds
19	19.5	2				156" / 4-1/3 yds
18.5	19	2				152" / 4-1/4 yds
18	18.5	2				148" / 4-1/8 yds
17.5	18	2	163" 4-5/8 yards	For smallest number of pieces: Cut these lengths of fabric LOF unless the fabric design must be cut WOF.	8 WOF strips needed for 9 yard (324") strip	144" / 4 yds
17	17.5	2				140" / 4 yds
16.5	17	2				136" / 3-7/8 yds
16	16.5	2				132" / 3-2/3 yds
15.5	16	2				128" / 3-5/8 yds
15	15.5	2				124" / 3-1/2 yds
14.5	15	2				120" / 3-1/3 yds
14	14.5	2 or 3				116" / 3-1/4 yds
13.5	14	3				112" / 3-1/8 yds
13	13.5	3				108" / 3 yds
12.5	13	3				104" / 3 yds
12	12.5	3	110" 3-1/8 yards			100" / 2-7/8 yds
11.5	12	3				96" / 2-2/3 yds
11	11.5	3				92" / 2-5/8 yds
10.5	11	3 or 4				88" / 2-1/2 yds
10	10.5	4				84" / 2-1/3 yds
9.5	10	4	83" 2-1/3 yards			80" / 2-1/4 yds
9	9.5	4				76" / 2-1/8 yds
8.5	9	4 or 5				72" / 2 yds
8	8.5	5				68" / 2 yds
7.5	8	5	67" 1-7/8 yards			64" / 1-7/8 yds
7	7.5	5				60" / 1-2/3 yds
6.5	7	6	57" 1-5/8 yards			56" / 1-5/8 yds
6	6.5	6				52" / 1-1/2 yds
5.5	6	7	50" 1-1/2 yards			48" / 1-1/3 yds
5	5.5	7				44" / 1-1/4 yds
4.5	5	8 or 9	45" / 1-1/4 yds			40" / 1-1/8 yds
4	4.5	9 or 10	41" / 1-1/8 yds	For smallest # of pieces, cut WOF unless the design must be cut LOF.		36" / 1 yd
3.5	4	11	37" / 1-1/8 yds			32" / 7/8 yd
3	3.5	12	33" / 1 yd			28" / 7/8 yd
2.5	3	14	30" / 7/8 yd			24" / 2/3 yd
2	2.5	16	28" / 7/8 yd			20" / 5/8 yd
1.5	2	21	26" / 3/4 yd			16" / 1/2 yd
1	1.5	28				12" / 1/3 yd

THE 1-HOUR QUILT TOP

Rectangle Box Quilts: Changing Size Chart

To make a size different from the standard pattern, use the table below for mother strip width, mother strip length, and yardage.

RECTANGLE BOX QUILT (MOTHER STRIP MAKES 2 QUILTS)

BED SIZE	BED DIMENSIONS H	BED DIMENSIONS W	QUILT SIZE RELATIVE TO BED SIZE	FINISHED SIZE OF QUILT H	FINISHED SIZE OF QUILT W	MSW (W/2) + .5 < H/2	HALF & HALF CONSTRUCTION — MOTHER STRIP LENGTH (H × 4) + 4	HALF & HALF — WHOLE CLOTH YARDS MSL / 36	HALF & HALF — YDS FOR STRIP SET	Y-SEAM CONSTRUCTION — MOTHER STRIP LENGTH (H × 4) + MSW + 4	Y-SEAM — WHOLE CLOTH YARDS MSL / 36	Y-SEAM — YDS FOR STRIP SET	COMMENTS
King	80	80	10" drop on sides & foot, 10" pillow wrap	100	100	USE SQUARE BOX PATTERN	SQUARE BOX PATTERN			SQUARE BOX PATTERN			MSW is too wide for 44" width, must build strip set
			10" drop on sides & foot, no pillow wrap	100	90	45.5	364	10-1/8	Calculate on Component Strip Yardage Chart page 73	409	11-3/8	Calculate on Component Strip Yardage Chart page 73	44" width makes one mother strip, leftover will not be enough for standard pattern Stripe quilt but may make a smaller quilt or can be used for backing
			Top only (square)	80	80	USE SQUARE BOX PATTERN	SQUARE BOX PATTERN			SQUARE BOX PATTERN			
			Top below pillows (Horizontal rectangle)	80	100	40.5	USE SQUARE BOX PATTERN			SQUARE BOX PATTERN			
Queen	80	60	10" Drop on sides & foot, 10" pillow wrap	80	80	30.5	244	6-7/8		274	7-5/8		
			10" Drop on sides & foot, no pillow wrap	80	80	40.5	404	11-1/4		454	12-5/8		44" width makes 1 mother strip, leftover makes 1 standard pattern Stripe quilt or backing
			Top only	60	80	40.5	364	10-1/8		409	11-3/8		
			Top below pillows	60	60	30.5	324	9		364	10-1/8		
Double	75	54	10" Drop on sides & foot, 10" pillow wrap	95	74	37.5	384	10-2/3		431.5	12		
			10" Drop on sides & foot, no pillow wrap	85	74	37.5	344	9-5/8		386.5	10-3/4		
			Top only	75	54	27.5	304	8-1/2		341.5	9-1/2		
			Top below pillows	60	54	USE SQUARE BOX PATTERN				SQUARE BOX PATTERN			
Twin	75	39	10" Drop on sides & foot, 10" pillow wrap	95	59	30	384	10-2/3		431.5	12		44" width makes 2 mother strips, can make 4 box quilts or stripe quilts
			10" Drop on sides & foot, no pillow wrap	85	59	30	344	9-5/8		386.5	10-3/4		
			Top only	75	39	20	304	8-1/2		341.5	9-1/2		
			Top only below pillows	55	39	20	224	6-1/4		251.5	7		
Crib / Baby	54	45		54	45	23	220	6-1/8		247	6-7/8		
	45	36		45	36	18.5	184	5-1/8		206.5	5-3/4		

Half & Half Construction

1. Prepare the mother strip

Standard Pattern: The mother strip is 324" (9 yards) long and 29-1/2" wide.

Whole-cloth fabric: Follow the instructions on page 32. Tear the fabric into two strips, 29-1/2" x 14-1/2" wide. Use the 29-1/2" strip for this mother strip, use the 14-1/2" strip for a Stripe quilt.

Strip set: Build an asymmetrical strip set 29-1/2" wide.

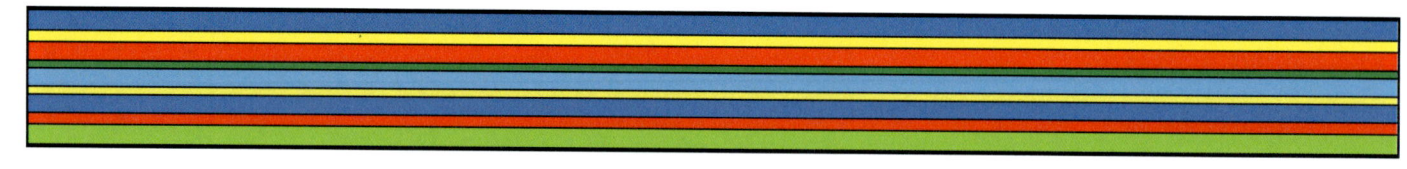

2. Cut the mother strip into quarter sections

Fold the mother strip in half, then in half again. Tear or cut across it at the folds to make four quarter sections 81" long. This is a rough cut for now — you'll even up the lengths, if necessary, a bit later on.

If you cut (rather than tore) the quarter sections, square up their ends before you fold and cut the triangles in the next step. If you tore them, the pieces should be on-grain and the ends square. If they're not, iron them square, rather than trim them.

Group the quarter sections into two pairs, Pair A and Pair B.

PAIR A

PAIR B

Square off each end of the quarter section by aligning edges to the mat and ruler.

2A. Strip sets only: Redirect seams

In each pair, press the seams on the quarter sections in opposite directions. The alternating directions will allow you to interlock seams at the corners when you assemble the triangles and trapezoids.

PAIR A   PAIR B

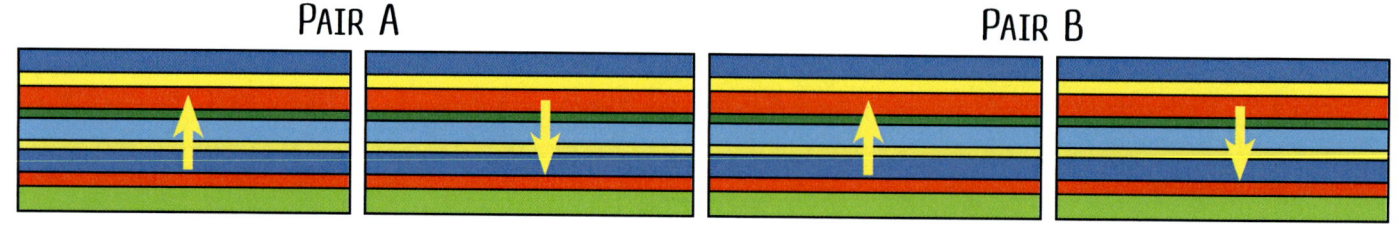

38   THE 1-HOUR QUILT TOP

3. Cut the quarter sections into trapezoids and triangles

Fold the ends of each quarter section diagonally as shown below. The end of the quarter strip should align with its outside edge. Pin the raw edges and the fold securely (photo 2, page 30).

Pair A Quarter Sections: Fold the end diagonally UP to the top edge.

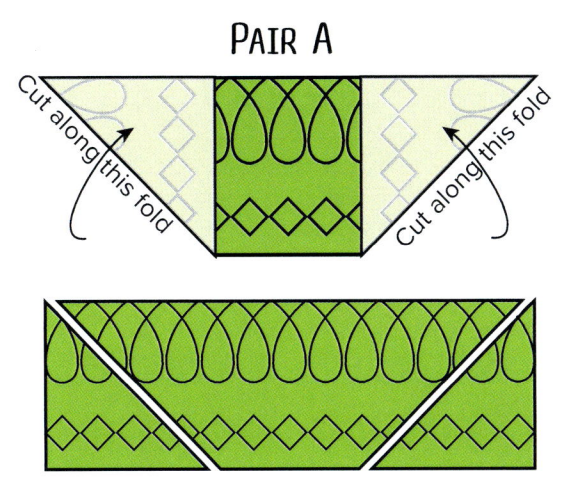

Pair B Quarter Sections: Fold the end diagonally DOWN to the bottom edge.

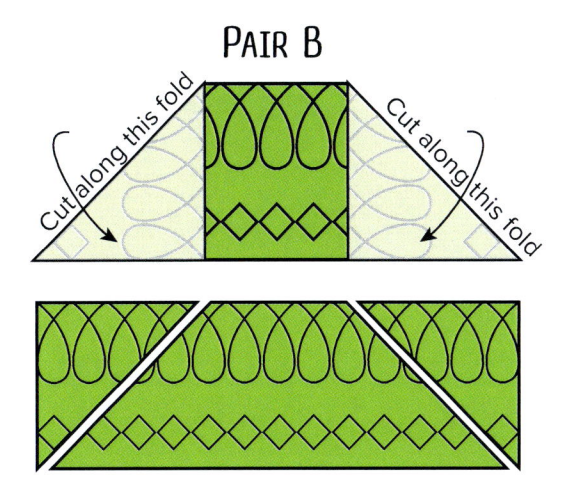

Cut along the fold (photo 3, page 30). Each quarter section is now one trapezoid and two triangles.

4. Check that both trapezoids in each pair are the same size

Stack each pair of trapezoids on top of one another. Line up one diagonal edge, the top edge and the bottom edge. Pin the edges and any lines and/or seams that should line up.

If one trapezoid is longer than the other, trim the larger trapezoid to match the smaller one so that the two trapezoids are the same size. Use scissors or a rotary cutter.

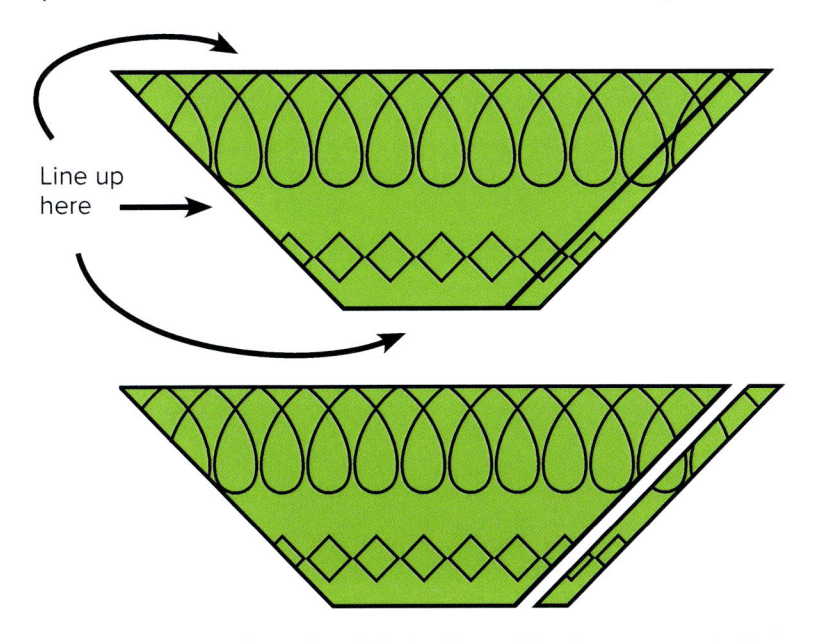

Line up here

Check the diagonal angle with the large V-ruler you made by taping rulers together. If any angle needs to be corrected to an accurate 45-degrees, fix it now. (In my experience, this is rarely necessary.)

RECTANGLE BOX QUILT: HALF & HALF CONSTRUCTION 39

5A. Swap the triangles: Whole-cloth fabric

Now exchange the triangles and the trapezoids. When you're done, all the pieces in each group will have the same design on the outside edges, and you can see the box take shape.

Group the Pair A trapezoids with the Pair B triangles to make the two halves of Quilt 1 (red arrows).

Group the Pair B trapezoids with the Pair A triangles to make the two halves of Quilt 2 (blue arrows).

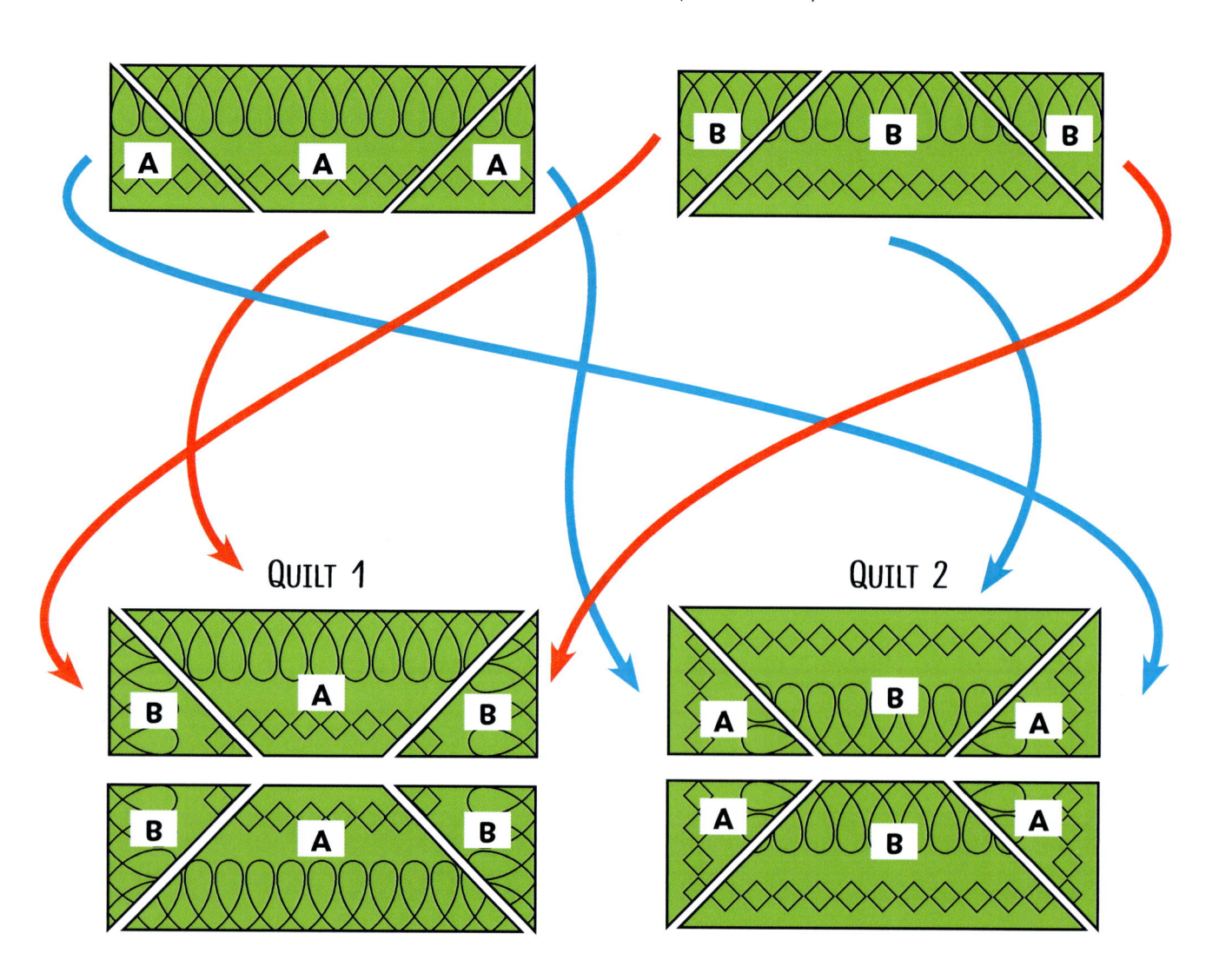

QUILT 1

QUILT 2

Stabilizing bias-cut edges

Put painter's tape along the edge about 1/2" back from the edge.
You can sew with the tape on without catching it in the seam, then remove it easily after sewing.

40   THE 1-HOUR QUILT TOP

5B. Swap the triangles: Strip sets

Combine the Pair A trapezoids with the Pair B triangles, and the Pair B trapezoids with the Pair A triangles. Pay attention to the directions that the seams were pressed (yellow arrows); adjoining section should have seams facing in opposite directions so they interlock to line up the seams. (Follow the numbers in the diagrams below for placement. Yellow arrows show directions of seams.)

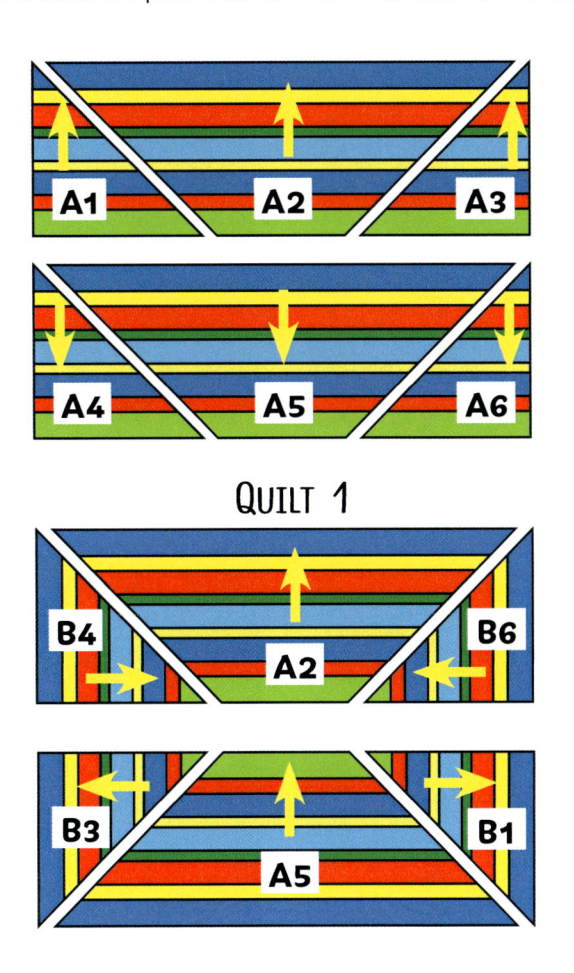

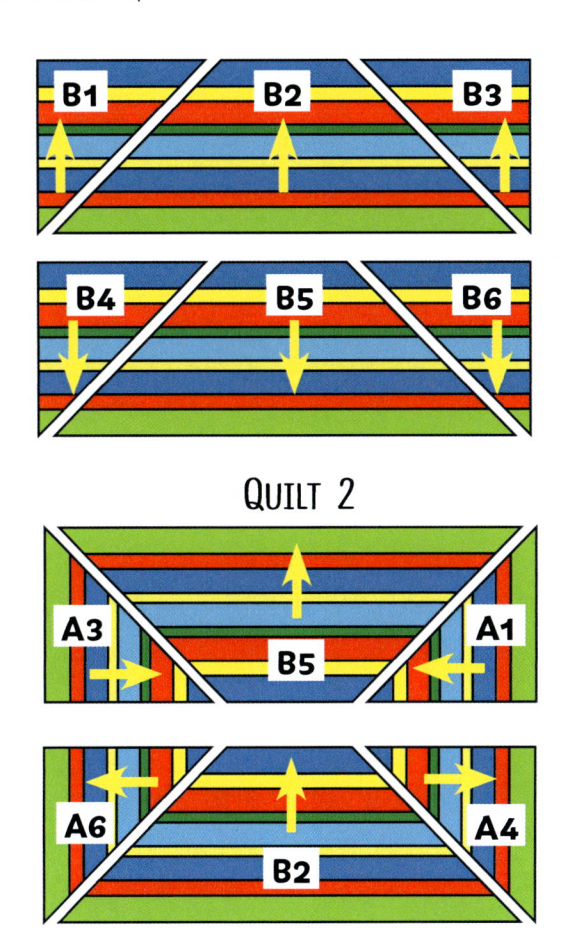

Quilt 1

Quilt 2

Making a Single Rectangle Box Quilt

The mother strip MUST be symmetrical (see page 20).

For Half & Half construction:

MSL: 2 times the finished height of the quilt, plus 2" seam allowances (H x 2) + 2

MSW: Any width as long as width is less than half the height of the quilt MSW < (H / 2)

Cutting: Cut the mother strip into two sections, then cut off triangles, one set up, one set down.

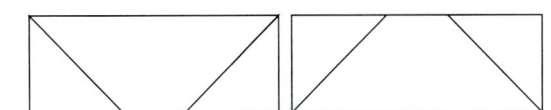

Assembly: Follow instructions on pages 38-42.

For Y-seam construction:

MSL: 2-1/2 times the finished height of the quilt, plus 2" seam allowances (H x 2.5) + 2

MSW: Any width as long as width is less than half the height of the quilt MSW < (H / 2)

Cutting: Cut as shown below. This corresponds to the instructions on pages 44-45.

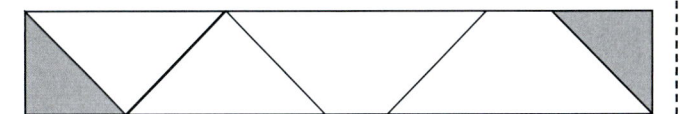

Assembly: Follow instructions on pages 44-47.

RECTANGLE BOX QUILT: HALF & HALF CONSTRUCTION

6. Sew the pieces together

6-1. For each quilt, pin the triangles to the trapezoids along the diagonal edges. Carefully match lines in the fabric so that they match at the mitered corner of the quilt. (Use the acupuncture pinning technique on page 31.)

Sew the diagonal seams.

6-2. After you sew the triangles to the trapezoids, the center edge of the trapezoid will extend out about 1/2" because of the width lost in the seam allowances. Trim this even with the edges of the triangles.

6-3. Now sew the two halves of each quilt together. Pin connecting lines between the triangles first, working toward the center. Pin the diagonal seams so that the seam allowances face opposite directions and interlock. (If the center section doesn't quite fit, stretch the two halves together to ease in the difference and don't worry about matching the diagonal seams.)

Quilt 1

Quilt 2

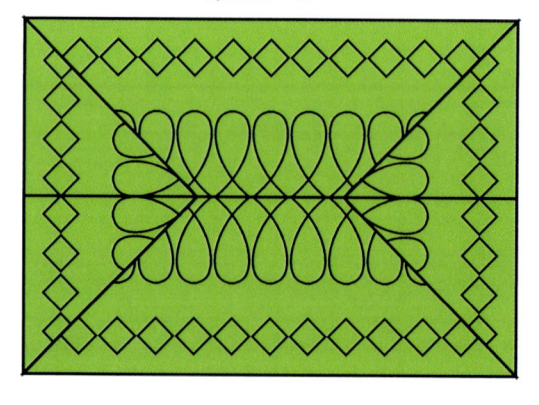

If you're working with a strip set, pin connecting seams between the triangles first, working toward the center. Again, use the interlock technique to accurately match up seams between the halves of the quilt. Sew the pieces together.

That's it, your Rectangle Box quilt tops are done!

Next: Quilt & Bind

(jump to page 64)

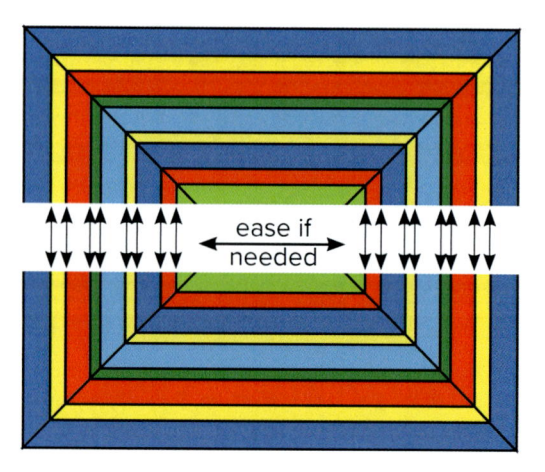

ease if needed

42 THE 1-HOUR QUILT TOP

The Sports Quilts

Two Rectangle Box quilts made from a whole-cloth fabric. The quilts are shorter than the standard pattern (but still rectangular) because I had less than the full 9 yards of fabric. It's easy to change the length of a Rectangle Box quilt — just make the quarter sections shorter or longer. Changing the width takes a bit more planning: the width of the mother strip must always be less than half the finished height of the quilt.

The Stripe quilt made from the removed strip is shown on page 62. I used it as backing for one of these quilts.

RECTANGLE BOX QUILT   43

Y-Seam Construction

In the Y-seam method, the short sides of the quilt are whole triangles. This eliminates the center seam through the end triangles that you had in the Half & Half method. The advantage of the Y-seam method is that it avoids breaking a large defined pattern that would be interrupted by a seam.

The Y-seam method requires extra length on the mother strip, a completely different approach to cutting it, and Y-seams to insert the end triangles.

1. Prepare the mother strip

The mother strip is 354" (10 yards) long and 29-1/2" wide.

Whole-cloth fabric: Follow the instructions on page 32. Tear the fabric into two strips, 29-1/2" x 14-1/2" wide. Use the 29-1/2" strip for this mother strip, use the 14-1/2" strip for a Stripe quilt.

Strip set: Build a strip set 29-1/2" wide.

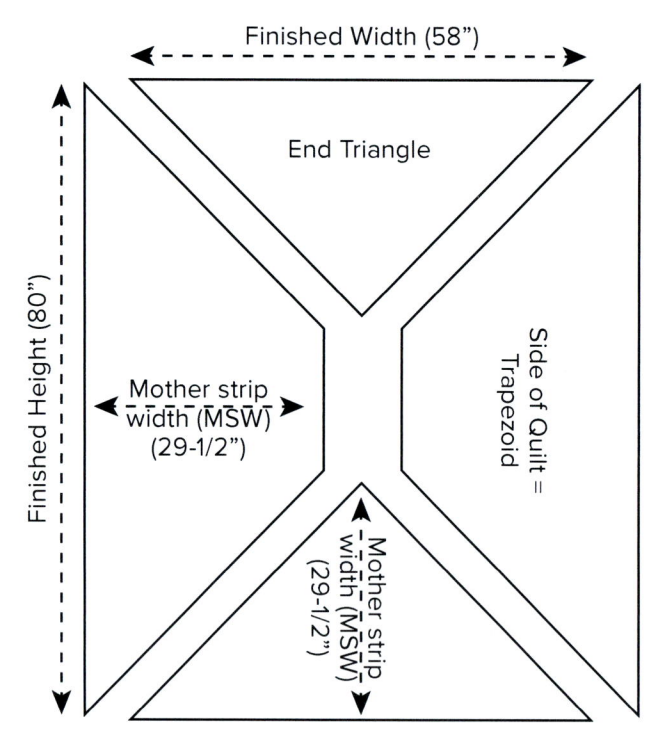

Layout of a Rectangular Box quilt using Y-seam construction. The measurements are the standard pattern dimensions.

2. Cut the mother strip into triangles and trapezoids

Make sure the length of the mother strip is long enough for all the triangles and trapezoids before you start cutting. You may want to mark out the pieces on the mother strip, just to be sure.

Use the pinning and cutting instructions on page 30.

In order for the quilts to lie flat, the pieces must be cut with accurate 90-degree and 45-degree angles, so check each angle with the large V ruler as you cut.

Cutting order: Square up the starting end of the mother strip so that the corners are 90-degrees to the sides of the strip. Cut all the triangles, then all the trapezoids.

Quilt 1 pieces = Pink   Quilt 2 pieces = Yellow

44   THE 1-HOUR QUILT TOP

Cut #1: Fold the left bottom corner diagonally up to the top edge of the mother strip. Cut along the diagonal fold. The small cut-off triangle is not used.

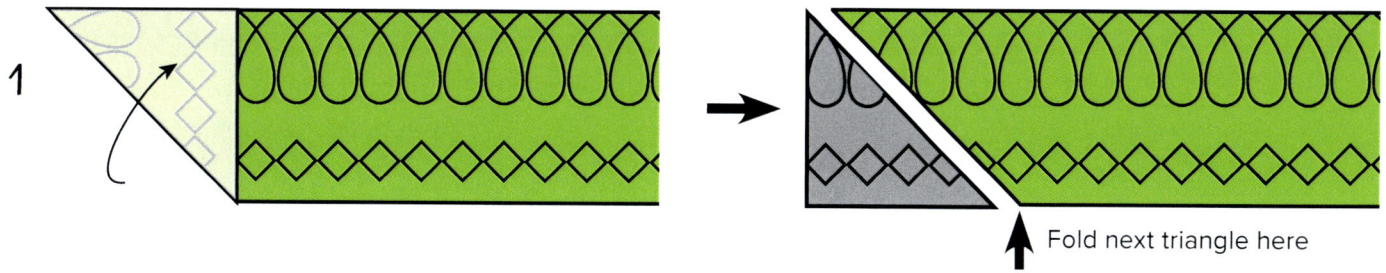

Fold next triangle here

Cuts #2-5, Triangles: Fold the new diagonal edge horizontally across the strip to make a large triangle. Fold exactly at the point of the wide angle where the previous diagonal cut stopped. Carefully align outside edge, seams and lines. Check the 45-degree angle with a ruler. Pin securely, then cut diagonally across the strip, using the diagonal edge as a guide.

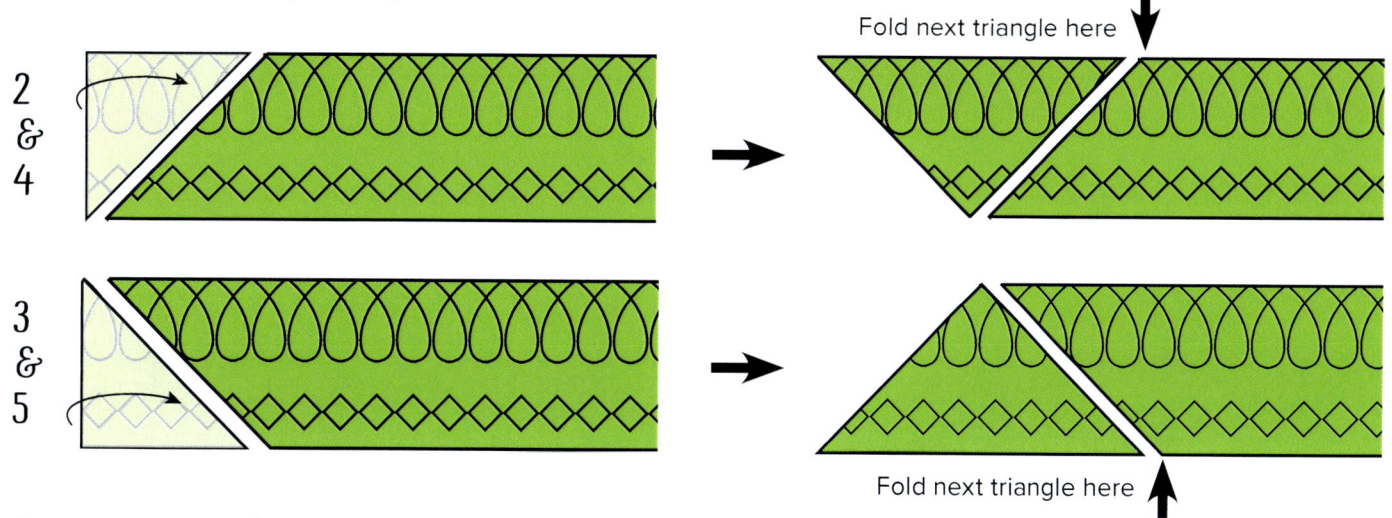

Fold next triangle here

Fold next triangle here

Cuts #6-9, Trapezoids: Fold the diagonal edge horizontally across the strip. The distance from the fold to the point of the trapezoid is 40-1/2" in the standard pattern. For other sizes, the distance is half the trapezoid, which is half height of the finished quilt plus 1/2". (H / 2) + 1/2

Line up all seams and lines. Pin securely, then cut across the strip using the diagonal edge as a guide.

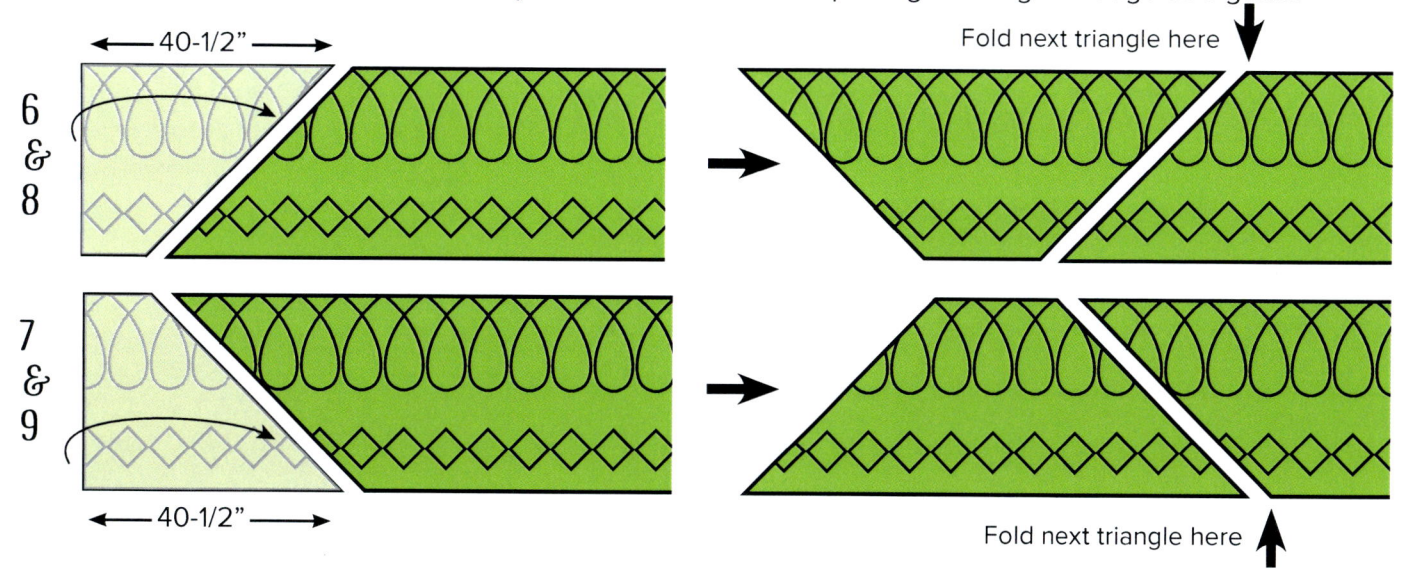

← 40-1/2" →

Fold next triangle here

← 40-1/2" →

Fold next triangle here

After all the cuts you will have four large triangles (two end triangles of Quilt 1, two end triangles of Quilt 2), four trapezoids (two sides of Quilt 1, two sides of Quilt 2), and two small triangles that are not used.

RECTANGLE BOX QUILT: Y-SEAM CONSTRUCTION

3. Check that the triangles and trapezoids are the same size

Gather the trapezoids and triangles into two groups, Quilt 1 and Quilt 2. The pieces in each group have the same design on the long edges of all pieces.

Stack the two trapezoids for Quilt 1 and check that they are the same length. If they are different, trim the length of the larger one to match the smaller one (see Step 4, page 39). Repeat for Quilt 2.

Stack the two triangles for Quilt 1 and check that they are the same size. If the triangles are different sizes, trim the larger one to match the smaller one (see below). Repeat for Quilt 2.

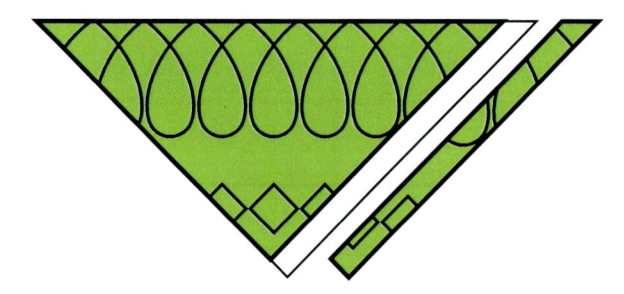

Keep in mind that trimming the triangles will not only make the width smaller, it will also shorten the triangle from the long side to the center point. You'll have to trim the trapezoids narrower to match the smaller width. However, DON'T trim the trapezoids until after you've assembled the pieces through Step 7 in the sewing instructions on the next page. Trim the trapezoids in Step 8.

3A. Extra step for strip sets: Redirect seams

Press the seams on the triangles in one direction and the seams on the trapezoids in the opposite direction. The alternating directions let you interlock seams at the corners.

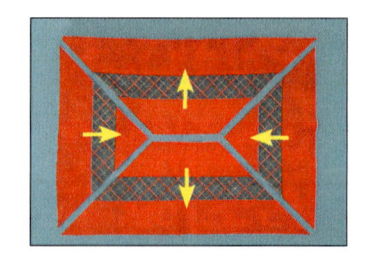

4. Sew the pieces together: Y-seam construction

Note: If you have sewn Y-seams in the past, the order of sewing these Y-seams may be different from how you have done it. The steps I show here prioritize matching the diagonal lines at the mitered corners.

4-1. At the center point of the end triangles, mark the point where the two side seams will cross; use intersecting lines or a dot.

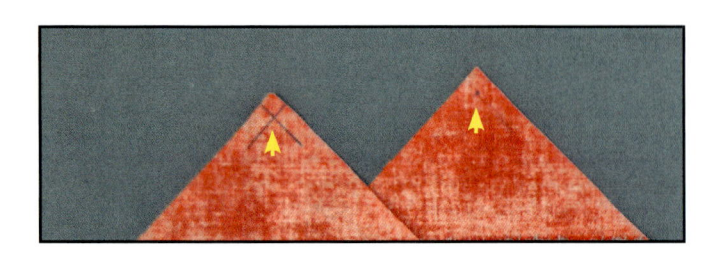

4-2. Pin a triangle to a trapezoid. Align lines in the fabric and/or interlock seams if you're using a strip set.

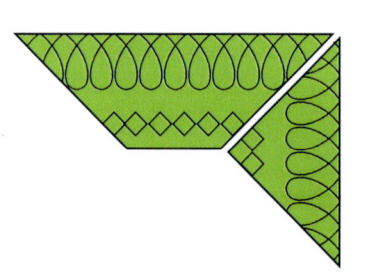

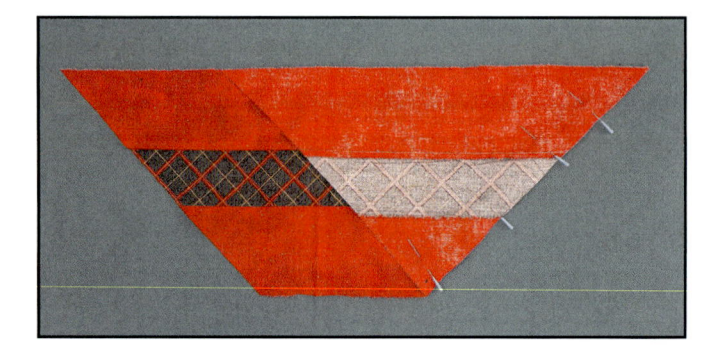

46   THE 1-HOUR QUILT TOP

4-3. Stitch the seam precisely to the mark at the corner of the triangle, then backstitch. (Backstitching is essential!)

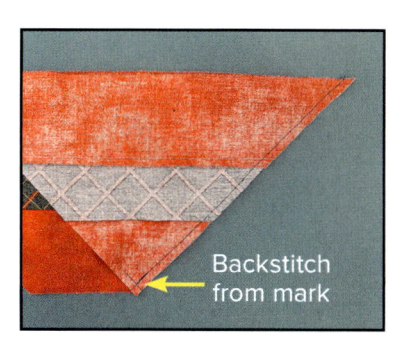

Backstitch from mark

4-4. Pin the other trapezoid to the other side of the end triangle. Align lines in the fabric; interlock seams if you're using a strip set.

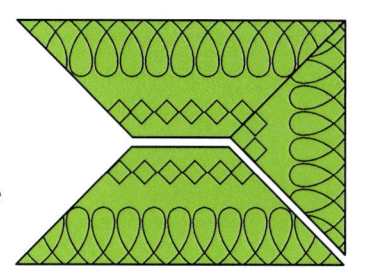

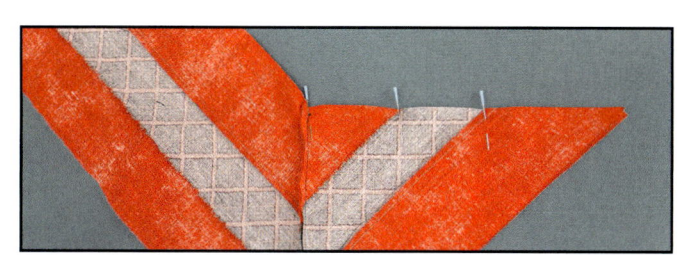

4-5. Stitch along this diagonal edge precisely to the end of the previous seam, then backstitch. Make sure not to stitch into the fold or stitches of the previous seam.

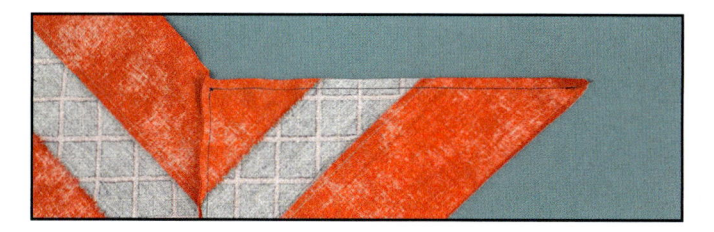

4-6. Repeat Steps 4-3 to 4-5 with the other triangle on the other ends of the trapezoids. You'll have a box with an unsewn seam in the middle.

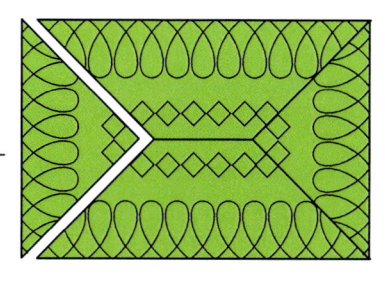

4-7. Fold the triangles into the space between the trapezoids. Line up the edges of the trapezoids. Trim the seam allowance along the short side of the trapezoids to 1/4" (Step 6-2, page 42).

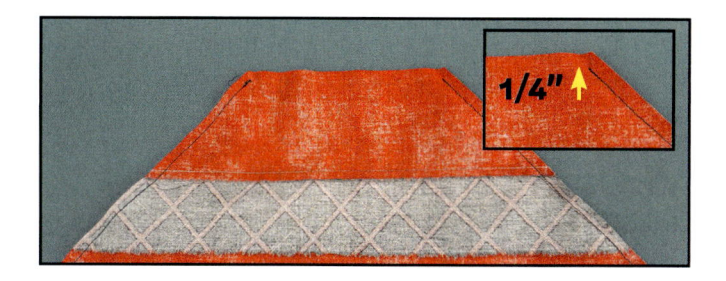

1/4"

4-8. Stitch across the short side of the trapezoids between the ends of the of the side seams. Stop and start exactly at the point of the stitches and backstitch at each end point.

4-9. Open the box. Press seams around the Y-seam, letting them fall in the direction they naturally lean.

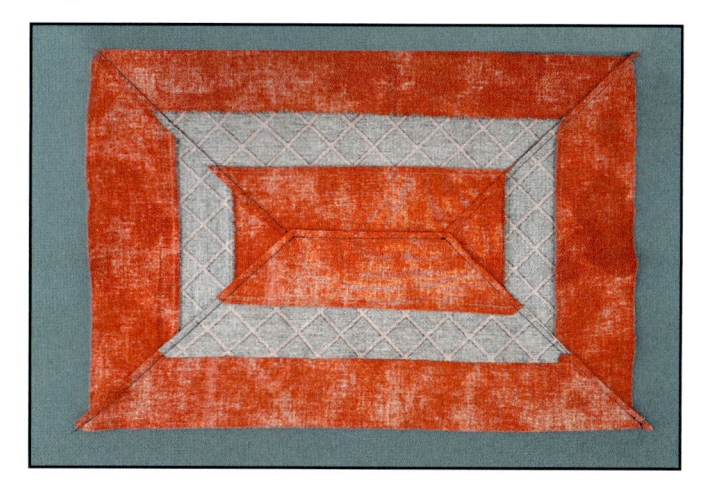

That's it, your Rectangle Box quilt top is done!

Next: Quilt & Bind

(jump to page 64)

RECTANGLE BOX QUILT: Y-SEAM CONSTRUCTION   47

The Blue Daisy Quilts

As I was choosing fabrics for other quilts, the blue daisy fabric was sitting at the side of the table. It kept calling my attention to fabrics I had rejected from other projects. Without even realizing it, I had stacked up these fabrics together. It's almost as if the blue daisy fabric chose them for me!

The second quilt is smaller because I didn't measure the mother strip before I cut and I ended up short on the last triangle. I had to cut down three other triangles to match the small one. Lesson learned — learn from my mistake!

You can see the strip set and planning chart for these quilts on page 78.)

48   THE 1-HOUR QUILT TOP

Square Box Quilts

Square Box quilts are built from triangles alone, no trapezoids. They are even easier to construct than Rectangle Box quilts, because they have only three straight seams. Take care in the cutting process to cut the triangles accurately.

The standard pattern here makes two 58" x 58" Square Box quilts. For different sizes, use the *Changing Size for Square Box Quilts*, page 51. If you want to make a single Square Box quilt, the instructions are also on page 51.

Materials for the Standard Pattern

Whole-cloth fabric: This table gives the mother strip dimensions and yardage for the standard pattern. The yardage makes three quilts; the removed strip of fabric makes a Stripe quilt, page 63.

MOTHER STRIP LENGTH (MSL):	270" (7-1/2 yards)	Note: These are minimums. Make the strip a bit longer for insurance.
MOTHER STRIP WIDTH (MSW):	29-1/2"	

Strip set: Build an asymmetrical strip set. Follow fabric selection guidelines on pages 20-23. This makes two quilts; there is no third quilt because you build the strip, rather than reduce the width of yardage.

▶ **Binding:** 1/2 yard for each 58" x 58" quilt. Refer to the Binding Chart on page 66 for different sizes.

▶ **Backing:** 1-3/4 yards of Minkee 60" or 90" wide for each quilt
OR 3-1/2 yards quilting fabric 44" wide for each quilt
Refer to the Backing Yardage Chart on page 68 for different sizes.

▶ **Batting:** Hobbs Heirloom Premium Fusible 80/20
1 Queen size roll will make two quilts 58" x 58" with some piecing.
If you use Minkee for backing, batting is optional

▶ **Thread:** to match fabric, for assembly and for quilting

The blue daisy fabric. The diamond stripe is part of the design.

SQUARE BOX QUILTS 49

Square Box Quilt: Standard Pattern Strip Set Yardage Chart

MSL = 270" (7-1/2 YDS)		IF CUTTING LOF		IF CUTTING WOF	
STRIP WIDTH		# OF LOF STRIPS YOU CAN CUT ACROSS WOF	YARDAGE NEEDED TO CUT LOF (INCHES & YDS)	# OF WOF STRIPS TO CUT	YARDAGE NEEDED TO CUT WOF (INCHES & YDS)
FINISHED STRIP WIDTH	CUT WIDTH	WOF = 43" (44" MINUS SELVAGES) (INCLUDES SEAM ALLOWANCES FOR JOINING STRIP ENDS)			
21	21.5	2	118" 3-1/3 yards		151 / 4-1/4 yds
20.5	21	2			147 / 4-1/8 yds
20	20.5	2			144 / 4 yds
19.5	20	2			140 / 4 yds
19	19.5	2			137 / 3-7/8 yds
18.5	19	2			133 / 3-3/4 yds
18	18.5	2			130 / 3-2/3 yds
17.5	18	2			126 / 3-1/2 yds
17	17.5	2			123 / 3-1/2 yds
16.5	17	2			119 / 3-1/3 yds
16	16.5	2			116 / 3-1/4 yds
15.5	16	2			112 / 3-1/8 yds
15	15.5	2			109 / 3 yds
14.5	15	2			105 / 3 yds
14	14.5	2 or 3			102 / 2-7/8 yds
13.5	14	3	79" 2-1/4 yards		98 / 2-3/4 yds
13	13.5	3			95 / 2-2/3 yds
12.5	13	3			91 / 2-5/8 yds
12	12.5	3			88 / 2-1/2 yds
11.5	12	3			84 / 2-1/3 yds
11	11.5	3			81 / 2-1/4 yds
10.5	11	3			77 / 2-1/4 yds
10	10.5	4	59" 2-1/3 yards		74 / 2-1/8 yds
9.5	10	4			70 / 2 yds
9	9.5	4			67 / 1-7/8 yds
8.5	9	4 or 5			63 / 1-3/4 yds
8	8.5	5	67" 1-2/3 yards		60 / 1-2/3 yds
7.5	8	5			56 / 1-5/8 yds
7	7.5	5			53 / 1-1/2 yds
6.5	7	6	40" 1-1/8 yards		49 / 1-1/2 yds
6	6.5	6			46 / 1-3/8 yds
5.5	6	7	34" 1 yard		42 / 1-1/4 yds
5	5.5	7			39 / 1-1/8 yds
4.5	5	8 or 9	29" / 7/8 yd		35 / 1 yds
4	4.5	9 or 10	27" / 3/4 yd		32 / 7/8 yd
3.5	4	11	22" / 5/8 yd		28 / 7/8 yd
3	3.5	12	20" / 5/8 yd		25 / 3/4 yd
2.5	3	14	17" / 1/2 yd		21 / 2/3 yd
2	2.5	16	15" / 1/2 yd		18 / 1/2 yd
1.5	2	21	12" / 1/3 yd		14 / 1/2 yd
1	1.5	28	8" / 1/4 yd		11 / 1/3 yd

Notes (middle column): For smallest number of pieces: Cut these lengths of fabric LOF unless the fabric design must be cut WOF.

Notes (WOF column): 7 WOF strips needed for 236" (6-5/8 yds) strip

For smallest number of pieces, cut WOF unless the design must be cut LOF.

50 THE 1-HOUR QUILT TOP

Square Box Quilts: Changing Size Chart

To make a size different from the standard pattern, use the table below for mother strip width, mother strip length, and yardage.

SQUARE BOX (MOTHER STRIP MAKES 2 QUILTS)					
FINISHED HEIGHT-WIDTH	MOTHER STRIP WIDTH	MOTHER STRIP LENGTH	YARDAGE FOR WHOLE-CLOTH FABRIC	YARDAGE FOR STRIP SET
HW	(HW / 2) + .5	(HW X 4.5) + 4 OR (MSW X 9) + 4	MSL / 36	Refer to Component Strip Yardage Chart page 73
30	15.5	139	3-7/8	
35	18	161.5	4-1/2	
40	20.5	184	5-1/8	
45	23	206.5	5-3/4	
50	25.5	229	6-3/8	
55	28	251.5	7	
60	30.5	274	7-5/8	
65	33	296.5	8-1/4	
70	35.5	319	8-7/8	
75	38	341.5	9-1/2	
80	40.5	364	10-1/8	
85	43	386.5	10-3/4	
90	45.5	409	11-3/8	
95	48	431.5	12	
100	50.5	454	12-5/8	

Making a Single Square Box Quilt

The mother strip MUST be symmetrical (page 20), so that the triangles cut from each side are the same.

Mother strip width: Use the table above to get the MSW based on the Finished Height-Width.

Mother strip length: 5 times the mother strip width plus 2" seam allowances. (MSW x 5) + 2
(Another way to figure it: 2-1/2 times the Height-Width plus 2". (HW x 2.5) + 2
Add an extra 12" or so for "insurance."

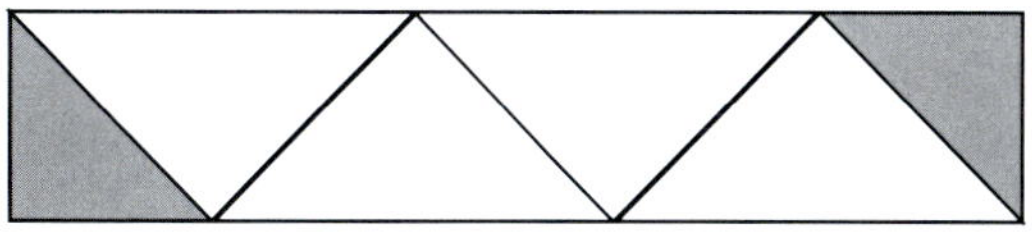

Cutting: Use the instructions on the next page, but cut only 4 triangles, as shown in the diagram here.

Assembly: The rest of the instructions are the same.

SQUARE BOX QUILTS

Making Square Box Quilts

1. Prepare the mother strip

Standard Pattern: The mother strip is 236" (6-5/8 yards) long and 29-1/2" wide.

Whole-cloth fabric: Follow the instructions on page 32. Tear the fabric into two strips, 29-1/2" x 14-1/2" wide. Use the 29-1/2" strip for this mother strip, use the 14-1/2" strip for a Stripe quilt.

Strip set: Build an asymmetrical strip set 29-1/2" wide.

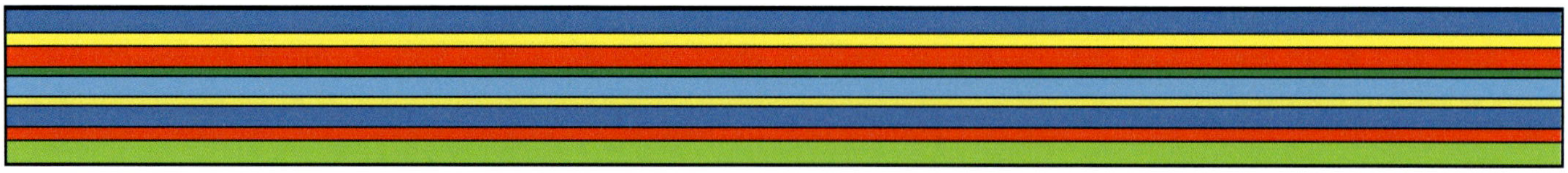

2. Check the mother strip dimensions (DON'T skip this step!)

Before you begin cutting, re-check the dimensions of the mother strip. This step is crucial when cutting triangles for a square quilt. Because the proportions of a right isosceles triangle are fixed, any change in the size of the triangle, the mother strip length or the mother strip width will change the dimensions of all three, and that will impact the mother strip length.

The length should be at least 9 times the width to fit all the triangles plus the extra length. If the width is narrower than planned, you'll be okay, as long as the length is at least 9 times the width.

If the width is wider than you planned, the length of the triangles will be longer than planned and the mother strip may be too short. Use one of the fixes below.

Solution #1 (easiest): Reduce the width: remove some fabric from one or both sides of the mother strip.

Solution #2 (more complicated): If you have more fabric, add length to the end of the mother strip. If you're working with a strip set, it's best way to add fabric to each component strip, then sew the lengthwise seams. This will ensure smooth seams past the add-ons.

I didn't plan the Blue Daisy quilt to go in this room, but when I laid it out on the bed for an initial photograph, it fit perfectly in the decor!

52   THE 1-HOUR QUILT TOP

3. Cut the mother strip into triangles

Although assembling a Square Box quilt is simpler than a Rectangle Box quilt, cutting accurately is more important for the square quilt. Each section is a large quarter-square triangle, so in order for the quilt to come together and lie flat, the triangles must be cut with accurate 90-degree and 45-degree angles. Follow these cutting instructions to make sure the angles are true, the assembly simple and the final product gorgeous!

You'll cut the mother strip into 8 large triangles and 2 small triangles, one at each end (these are not used).

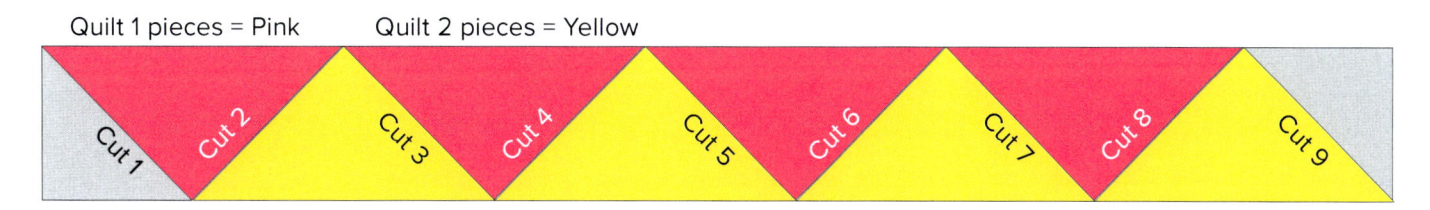

Quilt 1 pieces = Pink   Quilt 2 pieces = Yellow

Cut 1 · Cut 2 · Cut 3 · Cut 4 · Cut 5 · Cut 6 · Cut 7 · Cut 8 · Cut 9

Before beginning, square off the starting end of the mother strip. The corners should be accurate 90-degree angles. This is important for keeping the angles correct all through the cutting process.

Cut #1: Fold the left bottom corner diagonally up to the top edge of the mother strip. Pin securely, then cut along the diagonal fold (photos 2 & 3, page 30). The small cut-off triangle is not used.

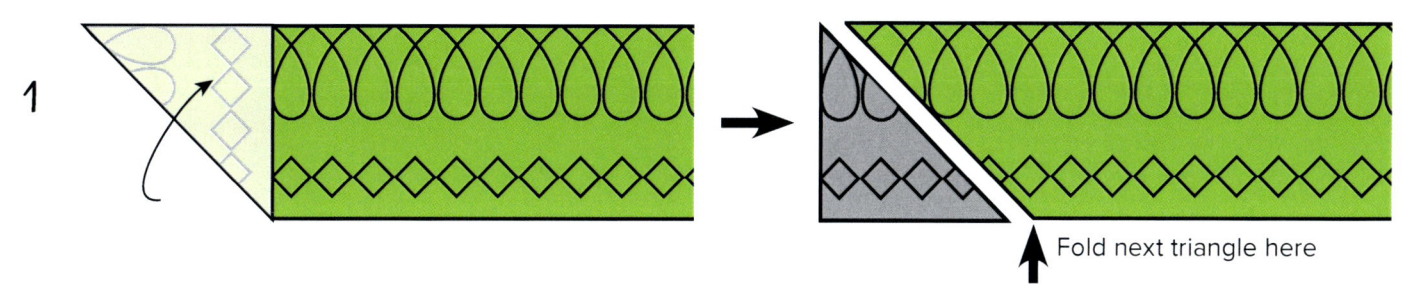

1

Fold next triangle here

All other cuts: Fold the new diagonal edge horizontally across the strip to make a large triangle. Fold exactly at the point of the wide angle where the previous diagonal cut stopped. Carefully align the outside edge, seams and lines. Check the 45-degree angle with the ruler. Pin securely, then cut diagonally across the strip, using the diagonal edge as a guide.

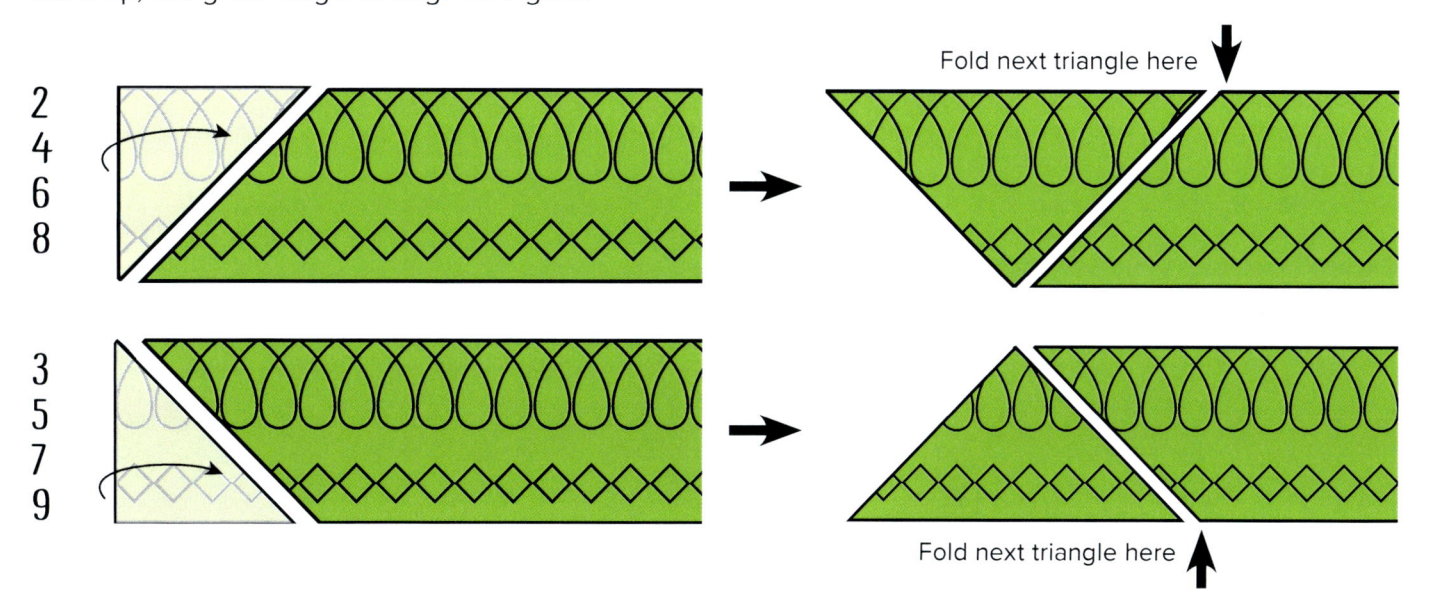

2
4
6
8

Fold next triangle here

3
5
7
9

Fold next triangle here

SQUARE BOX QUILTS 53

4. Fine-tune the triangles

Gather the triangles into two groups for Quilt 1 and Quilt 2. The pieces in each group have the same design on the long edges of the triangles.

Stack all four of the triangles for Quilt 1 and check them for size. If the triangles are different sizes, put the largest one on the bottom and the smallest one on top. Line up all the lines and seams along one short side of the triangles and pin them securely. (Be sure to line up the seam, not the seam allowance.) Smooth out the triangles across their width, then pin and align the seams and lines on the other side at the edge of the smallest triangle (which is on the top).

Place the large V-ruler over the stack and align it to the seams and sides of the triangles (see page 27). Square up the triangles and make them all the same size. Repeat for Quilt 2.

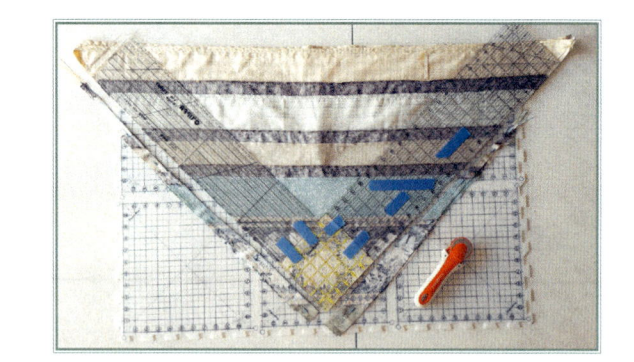

4A. Extra step for strip sets: Redirect seams

On two of the triangles in each group, press the seams in the opposite direction. This will allow you to interlock the seams when you join the triangles, assuring clean points at the mitered corners.

5. Sew the triangles together

For each quilt, lay out the four triangles. If you're using a strip set, lay pieces with seams in alternating directions. At this point, check for the Tent or Wings problem on the next page. (DON'T SKIP THIS!)

Pin together the edges that you'll sew to make each half of the quilt. (DO pin! Because the triangles are all the same, it's easy to sew the wrong edges together, which could reverse the alternating seams and set the seams in the same, rather than opposing, directions when you add the other half.)

Sew together the two pairs of pinned triangles to make half of the quilt.

Sew together the two halves. Match and interlock the seams at the center of each half. Then work outward, matching lines and seams. (Follow instructions on page 31 for interlocking, sewing and pinwheeling seams.)

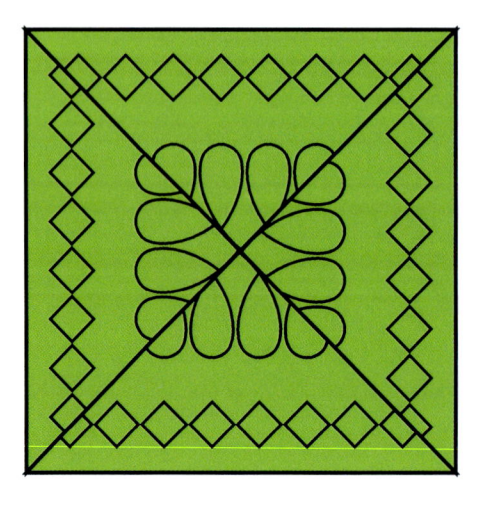

That's it, your Square Box quilt tops are done!

Next: Quilt & Bind

(jump to page 64)

54 THE 1-HOUR QUILT TOP

What Could Possibly Go Wrong?

Oh No! The mother strip is too short!

You get to the last cut and discover that there's not enough fabric for the last triangle. What now?

Option 1: You can make one quilt from the four full-size triangles that you have. Then, for the second quilt, cut the largest triangle you can from the end of the mother strip, and cut down the other three triangles to make smaller quilt (that's what happened with the second quilt on page 48). Be sure to conform the sizes of the triangles as shown on the previous page so that all the triangles will fit. Otherwise, you'll have to trim the second quilt down even further to correct the angles and make the quilt lie flat. (See "Tents" and "Wings" below.)

Option 2: If you have more fabric, lengthen the mother strip and enlarge the last triangle. A lot more work, but if you really want that full-size second quilt, this is the only option.

Oh No! There's a tent in the middle of my quilt! OR
The corners of my quilt are flapping like wings!

Both of these problems are the result of not having accurate 90-degree points on your triangles. If you don't discover the problem until after the triangles are sewn together, you'll need to take them apart. Either way, re-cut the triangles to fix the problem.

Tent: If there's a tent in the middle, it means that the angle at the center of the triangle was less than 90 degrees (red line). The outer edges pull together tighter than they should have, so the center pops up.

The fix: Take apart the four triangles, use the large V ruler to re-cut the center angle (see previous page) so it is accurately 90 degrees (blue line). Then, re-assemble the triangles.

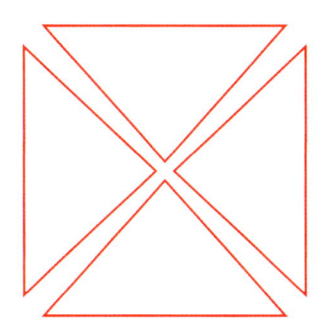

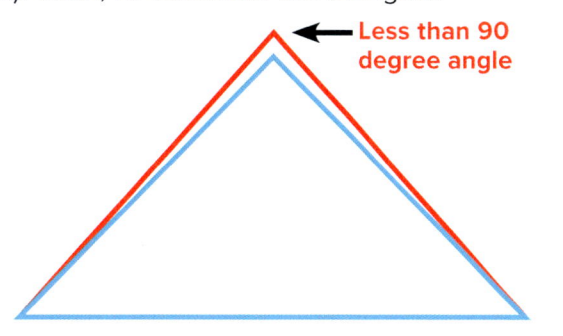

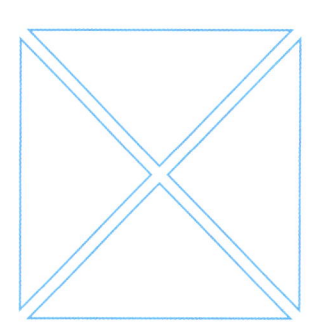

Wings: If there is excess width at the at the corners that needs to be taken in, it means that the triangle point at the center of the quilt had an angle of more than 90 degrees (red line).

The fixes: Fix 1: Lay the quilt flat, face down. Working from the center outward, take in the slack equally at each corner, until the quilt lies flat. Pin and press along the new seam lines, then re-stitch each seam.
Fix 2: Take apart the four triangles along the pressed line. Use the large V ruler to re-cut the sides so the center is an accurate 90 degree angle (blue line). Then, re-assemble the triangles.

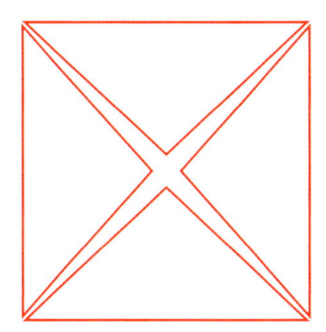

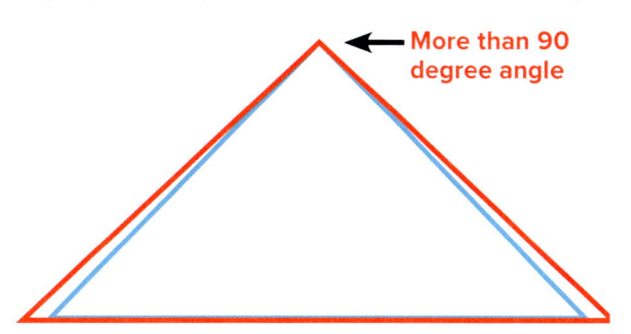

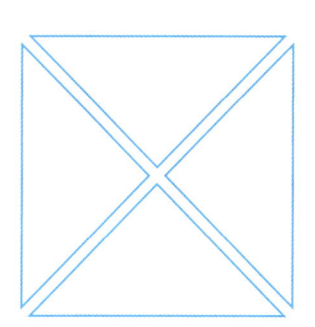

SQUARE BOX QUILTS 55

The Plaid Diamond Quilt

This quilt is unique among the quilts in this book because the "focal" print is not border print or large print but a wonderful multicolor woven plaid. I had very limited amounts of both the plaid and the stripe, so there was only enough for one small quilt. Using it in a DITS quilt made it look as though I had a lot more of it; cut into all eight triangles, it appears eight times in the quilt. You can see the strip set and planning chart on page 77.

Diamond-in-the Square Quilts

For Diamond-in-the-Square (DITS) quilts, the mother strip is cut into eight triangles, the same as in a square quilt. But, instead of making two square quilts of four triangles each, you use all eight triangles in each quilt, placed on the diagonal instead of on the square. The standard pattern here makes two quilts 58" x 58". For different sizes, use the table on page 59. If you want to make only one quilt, instructions are also on page 59.

Keep in mind this difference between Square Box and DITS quilts: Square Box quilts have the edges of the mother strip around the OUTSIDE of the quilts, while a DITS quilt places the edges of the mother strip in the MIDDLE of the diamond. Depending on whether the adjoining fabrics blend or contrast, you may or may not see a strong line along the diagonal where the bases of the triangles meet.

When you assemble a DITS quilt, all of the outside edges will be on the bias, so they can stretch easily. To help keep the quilt square, stick painter's tape about 1/2" back from the bias-cut edges as you cut the triangles and keep it there through the assembly process until you're ready to quilt. Also, using fusible batting will help keep the quilt top from stretching when you quilt it.

Materials for the Standard Pattern

Whole-cloth fabric: This table gives the mother strip dimensions and yardage for the standard pattern. Since the MSW is 21", which is half the 42"-44" width of quilting fabric, the yardage will make two quilts. Each half of the yardage is one mother strip that will make one complete DITS quilt.

MOTHER STRIP LENGTH (MSL):	187" (5-1/4 yards rounds up to 189")	*Note: These are minimums. Make*
MOTHER STRIP WIDTH (MSW):	21"	*the strip a bit longer for insurance.*

Strip set: Build an asymmetrical strip set. Follow fabric selection guidelines on pages 20-23.
A strip set will make one DITS quilt.

- **Binding:** 1/2 yard for each 58" x 58" quilt. Refer to the Binding Chart on page 66 for different sizes.

- **Backing:** 1-3/4 yards of Minkee 60" or 90" wide for each quilt
  OR 3-1/2 yards quilting fabric 44" wide for each quilt
  Refer to the Backing Yardage Chart on page 68 for different sizes.

- **Batting:** Hobbs Heirloom Premium Fusible 80/20
  1 Queen size roll will make two quilts 58" x 58" with some piecing.
  If you use Minkee for backing, batting is optional

- **Thread:** to match fabric, for assembly and for quilting

Diamond-in-the-Square: Standard Pattern Strip Set Yardage Chart

MSL = 187" (5-1/4 YDS)		IF CUTTING LOF			IF CUTTING WOF	
STRIP WIDTH		# OF LOF STRIPS YOU CAN CUT ACROSS WOF	YARDAGE NEEDED TO CUT LOF (INCHES & YDS)		# OF WOF STRIPS TO CUT	YARDAGE NEEDED TO CUT WOF (INCHES & YDS)
FINISHED STRIP WIDTH	CUT WIDTH	WOF = 42" (44" MINUS SELVAGES, INCLUDES SEAM ALLOWANCES FOR JOINING STRIP ENDS)				
20.5	21	2				105" / 3yds
20	20.5					103" / 2-7/8 yds
19.5	20					100" / 2-7/8 yds
19	19.5					98" / 2-3/4 yds
18.5	19					95" / 2-5/8 yds
18	18.5					93" / 2-5/8 yds
17.5	18		94" 2-3/4 yards			90" / 2-1/2 yds
17	17.5					88" / 2-1/2 yds
16.5	17					85" / 2-3/8 yds
16	16.5					83" / 2-1/3 yds
15.5	16					80" / 2-1/4 yds
15	15.5				For smallest number of pieces: Cut these lengths of fabric LOF unless the fabric design must be cut WOF.	78" / 2-1/4 yds
14.5	15					75" / 2-1/8 yds
14	14.5	2 or 3				73" / 2-1/8 yds
13.5	14	3				70" / 2 yds
13	13.5					68" / 2 yds
12.5	13					65" / 1-7/8 yds
12	12.5		63" 1-3/4 yards			63" / 1-3/4 yds
11.5	12					60" / 1-2/3 yds
11	11.5					58" / 1-5/8 yds
10.5	11	3 or 4			5 WOF strips needed for 187" (5-1/4 yds) strip	55" / 1-5/8 yds
10	10.5	4				53" / 1-1/2 yds
9.5	10		47" 1-1/3 yards			50" / 1-1/2 yds
9	9.5					48" / 1-1/3 yds
8.5	9	4 or 5				45" / 1-1/4 yds
8	8.5	5	38" 1-1/8 yards			43" / 1-1/4 yds
7.5	8					40" / 1-1/8 yds
7	7.5					38 / 1-1/8 yds
6.5	7	6	32" 7/8 yards		For smallest number of pieces, cut WOF unless the design must be cut LOF.	35" / 1 yd
6	6.5					33" / 1 yd
5.5	6	7	27" 3/4 yd			30" / 7/8 yd
5	5.5					28" / 7/8 yd
4.5	5	8 or 9	24" / 3/4 yd			25" / 3/4 yd
4	4.5	9 or 10	21" / 5/8 yd			23" / 2/3 yd
3.5	4	11	19 / 5/8 yd			20" / 5/8 yd
3	3.5	12	16" / 1/2 yd			18" / 2/3 yd
2.5	3	14	14" / 1/2 yd			15" / 1/2 yd
2	2.5	16	12" / 1/3 yd			13" / 3/8 yd
1.5	2	21	9" / 1/4 yd			10" / 1/3 yd
1	1.5	28	7" / 1/4 yd			8" / 1/4 yd

Diamond-in-the-Square Quilt: Changing Size Chart

To make a size different from the standard pattern, use the table below for mother strip width, mother strip length, and yardage.

MOTHER STRIP WIDTH & HEIGHT FOR DIAMOND-IN-THE-SQUARE QUILTS					YARDAGE FOR STRIP SET
FINISHED HW OF QUILT	MOTHER STRIP WIDTH	MOTHER STRIP LENGTH	YARDAGE FOR WHOLE-CLOTH FABRIC		
HW	(HW / 2) / 1.4) + .5	(MSW X 9) + 4	YARDS		
30	12	112	3-1/8	Yardage will make 3 mother strips	Calculate on Component Strip Set Yardage Chart, page 73
35	13	121	3-3/8	Yardage will make 3 mother strips	
40	15	139	3-7/8	Yardage will make 2 mother strips	
45	17	157	4-3/8	Yardage will make 2 mother strips	
50	19	175	4-7/8	Yardage will make 2 mother strips	
55	21	193	5-3/8	Yardage will make 2 mother strips	
60	22	202	5-5/8	Yardage will make 1 mother strip with leftover that could be used for a Stripe quilt	
65	24	220	6-1/8		
70	26	238	6-5/8		
75	28	256	7-1/8		
80	30	274	7-5/8		
85	31	283	7-7/8		
90	33	301	8-3/8		
95	35	319	8-7/8		
100	37	337	9-3/8		

Making a Single Diamond-in-the-Square Quilt

In the standard pattern the mother strip is used completely to make a single quilt, so all you have to do is follow the instructions. If you're using a strip set, just build the strip set to the mother strip width.

Mother strip width: Use the table above to get the width.

Mother strip length: Use the table above to get the length. You'll see in the table that in some cases the yardage will make more than one mother strip. Depending on the design of the fabric, you might be able to buy 1/2 or 1/3 the mother strip length, split it, then sew the pieces end-to-end for the full mother strip length.

Cutting: Use the instructions on the next page.

Assembly: The rest of the instructions are the same.

Making a Diamond-in-the-Square Quilt

1. Prepare the mother strip

Standard Pattern: The mother strip is 187" (5-1/4 yards) long and 21" wide.

Whole-cloth fabric: Follow the instructions on page 32. Tear the fabric into two strips 21" wide. Each strip will make one complete quilt.

Strip set: Build an asymmetrical strip set 21" wide.

2. Check the mother strip dimensions (DON'T skip this step!)

Before you begin cutting, re-check the dimensions of the mother strip. This step is crucial when cutting triangles for a DITS quilt. Because the proportions of a right isosceles triangle are fixed, any change in the size of either the triangle, the mother strip length or the mother strip width will change the dimensions of all three, and that will impact the mother strip length needed.

The length should be at least 9 times the width to fit all the triangles plus the extra length. You may want to mark out where you're going to cut the triangles, just to be sure they all fit.

3. Cut the mother strip into triangles

Cut the mother strip into triangles as shown in the diagram below. Follow the cutting instructions on page 53. Place painter's tape 1/2" from the bias edges to prevent stretching.

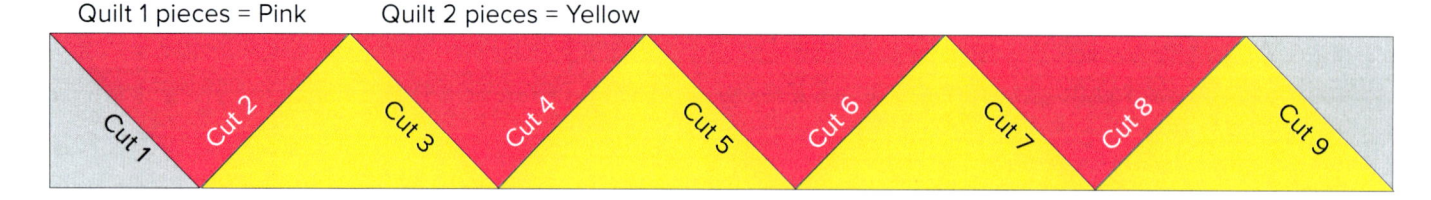

Quilt 1 pieces = Pink   Quilt 2 pieces = Yellow

4. Fine-tune the triangles

Stack all eight triangles. Check to make sure that they are all the same size and the 90-degree angle is accurate. If necessary, use the large V ruler to trim and square them up (see photo page 54). If eight is too many, do them in smaller batches, but use the same triangle as the template to trim each batch.

5. Sew the triangles together into squares

Group the triangles into two groups of four matching triangles. Sew together four pairs of a Group 1 with a Group 2 triangle to make four squares.

Does That Diagram Look Familiar?

If you think the diagram above is the same as the one for Square Box quilts, you're right. What's different with DITS quilts is that we had to arrive at the size of the triangles with a different calculation, because the triangle sits diagonally rather than horizontally within the DITS quilt. I've done all the math for you — just cut the mother strip the same as for a Square Box quilt, then assemble them as shown on the next page to make the diamond.

6. Audition different arrangements

Although you may have already decided on an arrangement you liked, take a moment to audition another possibility or two. Try rotating the squares, placing Group 1 triangles, then the Group 2 triangles in the center. A third option might be to arrange the squares in an X rather than a diamond.

6A. Extra step for strip sets: Redirect seams

Once you've decided which triangles will face the center of the diamond, re-press the seams in the opposite direction on two of the inner triangles so you can interlock the seams along the center lines when you assemble the blocks. (Take care not to stretch the triangles out of shape when you iron.)

7. Sew the squares together to make a diamond

Join pairs of squares to make two columns. (Double-check the placement of the triangles before you stitch, to make sure they are faced in the right direction and you are sewing along the correct side of the square.)

Join the two columns to make the diamond.

That's it, your Diamond-in-the-Square quilt tops are done!

Next: Quilt & Bind

(jump to page 64)

DIAMOND-IN-THE-SQUARE QUILTS   61

Stripe Quilts

This striped quilt top is the companion to the Rectangle Box quilts on page 34. I used this as the back of the second box quilt — it was a way to carry two quilts in one when I teach. I sent the first box quilt to my niece at college.

This stripe quilt is the companion to the Rectangle Box quilts on page 43.

The Stripe Quilt

The Stripe quilt is made from the fabric removed from whole-cloth border fabric when you reduce the width to prepare the mother strip. If you make the Rectangle Box or Square Box quilt from the standard pattern, the size of the Stripe quilt will be approximately the same as the other quilts. Use it as a third quilt top, or as backing for another quilt.

Materials for the Standard Pattern

- **Whole-cloth fabric:** You removed a strip of fabric 14-1/2" wide when you prepared the mother strip. Use that strip of fabric for the Stripe quilt.

- **Binding:** 1/2 yard for a 58" x 58" quilt, or 2/3 yard for a 58" x 80" quilt. Refer to the Binding Chart on page 66 for other sizes.

- **Backing:** Refer to the Backing Yardage Chart on page 68 for different sizes.

58" X 58" QUILT	58" X 80" QUILT
1-3/4 yards of Minkee 60" or 90" wide for each quilt OR 3-1/2 yards quilting fabric 44" wide for each quilt	2-1/3 yards of Minkee 60" wide for each quilt OR 1-3/4 yards of Minkee 90" wide for each quilt OR 3-1/2 yards quilting fabric 44" wide for each quilt

- **Batting:** Hobbs Heirloom Premium Fusible 80/20, 1 Queen size roll. If you made two Rectangle or Square Box quilts, the leftover from 2 Queen size rolls of batting will be enough for this quilt. If you use Minkee for backing, batting is optional.

- **Thread:** to match fabric, for assembly and for quilting

Fold and sew the strip

1. Fold the strip in half face-to-face lengthwise. Pin together the edges that will be the INNER stripe. Sew the layers together along the pinned edge. Trim 1/8" off the folded edge.

2. Open the double strip flat and press the seam to one side.

3. Fold the double strip in half lengthwise again. Pin together the layers along one edge. (Since this strip is symmetrical across its width it doesn't matter which side.) Sew the layers together along the pinned edge.

Trim 1/8" off the folded edge. Open the strip flat and press the seam to one side.

The Stripe quilt top is finished with just two seams!

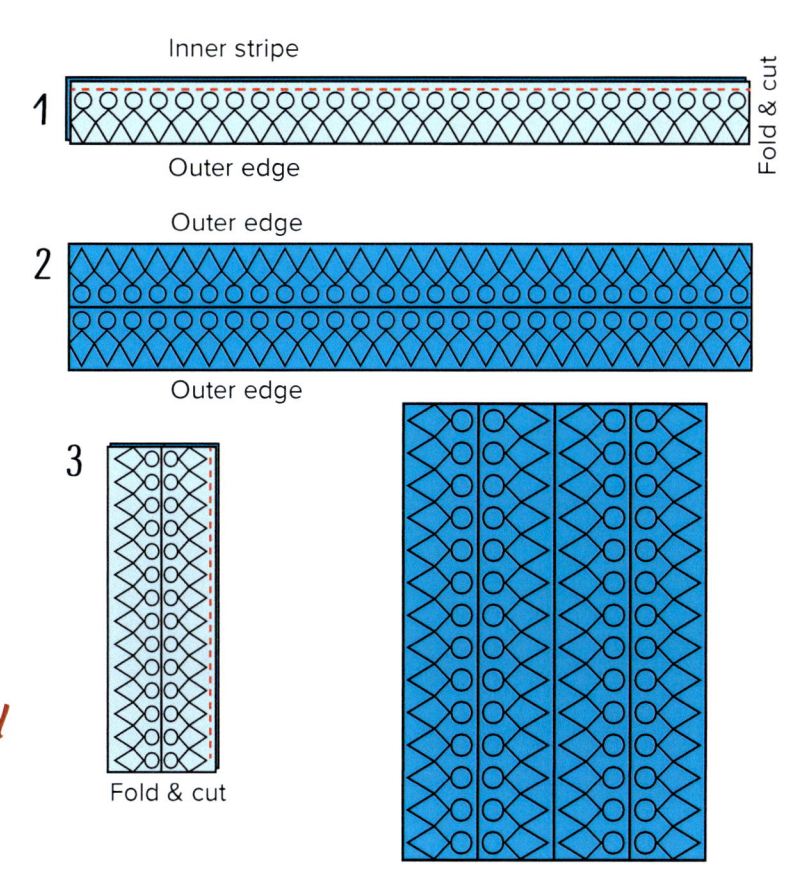

STRIPE QUILTS 63

Quilting a 1-Hour Quilt Top

Just to be clear, the title of this book is the 1-Hour Quilt TOP. So yes, it will require additional time to QUILT your quilt. But the good news is, it's easy and won't require a lot of time. You can do it yourself, even if your quilting skills are limited. It can be done on a regular domestic sewing machine. And, it requires no marking or free-motion quilting. It's helpful if you have a walking foot but that's not entirely necessary.

Batting

As I mentioned at the beginning of the book, I am a huge fan of fusible batting, and Hobbs Heirloom Premium Fusible 80/20 is my favorite. As far as I've been able to find, it's the only double-sided fusible batting on the market. Plus, it's repositionable, and lets go after the quilting is done, so the quilt is soft.

Fusible batting will keep the layers from shifting, even when you need to scrunch up the quilt to shove it through your sewing machine. If you don't have fusible batting, another option is fusing spray or powder.

If you need to piece batting together there's no need to sew fusible batting: just smash the pieces up tight against each other and fuse. A couple of pins at the edges will help keep everything stable until the layers are quilted. If you don't have fusible batting, whip-stitch pieces together.

Backing

If you're using regular quilting fabric, check the Backing Yardages Chart on page 68 for amounts.

Another option is Minkee. It comes in 60" width and 90" widths. This is one reason I sized the standard pattern to 58" x 80": it fits a Minkee backing in either direction. If you want to use Minkee to back your quilts, I recommend taking them to a longarm quilter. If you try to quilt Minkee on a domestic machine, it will slither and slide all over and drive you crazy! Batting is optional with Minkee; use batting for an extra-warm quilt or leave out the batting for a lighter-weight quilt.

Quilting

Start with lines: Begin by stitching along the straight lines of the fabric; stitch-in-the-ditch along seams of a strip set. Keep the feed dogs up as you do for regular sewing. A walking foot will help keep the layers from shifting. I often use a stiletto or even the tip of my seam ripper to help push the top layer forward. Start with the lines near the center and work your way out.

Fill in wide areas: Once you have the lines quilted in, wherever quilting lines are more than 2" apart, fill in the space with additional quilting. This doesn't need to be fancy — here are my two favorites.

Wavy lines: For narrower strips, a wavy line down the center is adequate. Use a regular foot and keep feed dogs up as you did for straight lines. If you are comfortable doing free-motion quilting, you can drop the feed dogs and use a free-motion foot for this.

Guided meandering: For large print fabrics, loosely outline the design with free-motion quilting. Use a free-motion foot with the feed dogs dropped.

The important thing to remember about the quilting is this: perfection is irrelevant. Get the quilting done without fussing over it and send the quilt out into the world to be used, loved and enjoyed. No one who receives one will judge the quilting: they will love it because you made it for them and that is ALL that matters.

Quilting Designs

Guided meandering: Loosely follow the design in the quilt. Stop at sharp points whenever you want to plot your next move. It's okay to backtrack, cross over lines, or stop and re-start.

Wavy lines: An S-curve chain my favorite patterns for filling in strips. Quilt an S-curve, then quilt a backwards S-curve. Repeat over and over. Stop between S's as frequently as needed to plan your next move, rearrange fabric, etc.

Carry the pattern into a point at corners.

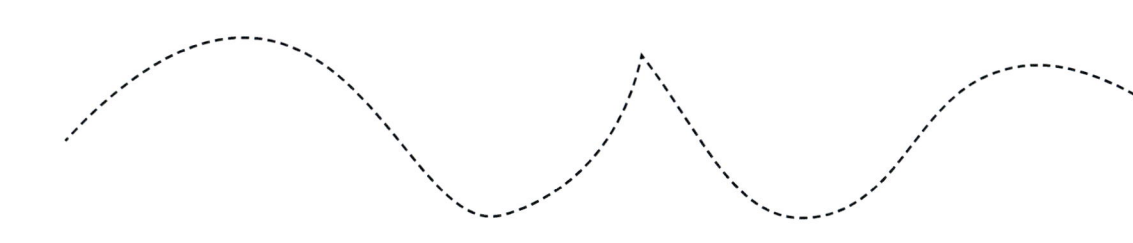

QUILTING A 1-HOUR QUILT

Binding Your Quilt

If you've been quilting a while, you've done lots bindings. But if you're new to quilting here are instructions. This is my favorite binding techniques. Have your bottle of school glue handy!

Binding Chart

This chart gives yardage and number of WOF strips to cut for binding a quilt, based on the linear inches of binding needed.

Linear inches of binding is comes from two times the height (H) plus two times the width (W) of the quilt. I add in 8" extra for mitering corners and overlapping ends. So,

(H x 2) + (W x 2) + 8" = Linear inches

Number of WOF strips is based on 40" usable length in a WOF strip. This accounts for removing selvages and joining strips with diagonal seams.

The width of the strips can range from 2-1/4" to 3". If the binding fabric matches the border fabric the strip can be as narrow as 2-1/4" and will finish to 1/4" wide. If it contrasts with the border fabric I prefer cutting it 3" wide so the binding finishes 1/2" wide.

# OF LINEAR INCHES NEEDED	# WOF STRIPS TO CUT	YDS IF CUT 2-1/4"	YDS IF CUT 3"
up to 40	1	1/8 yd	1/8 yd
41-80	2	1/8 yd	1/4 yd
81-120	3	1/4 yd	1/4 yd
121-160	4	1/4 yd	1/3 yd
161-200	5	3/8 yd	1/2 yd
201-240	6	3/8 yd	1/2 yd
Standard Pattern for Square Box & DITS = 240			
241-280	7	1/2 yd	5/8 yd
281-320	8	1/2 yd	2/3 yd
Standard Pattern for Rectangle Box & Stripe = 286			
321-360	9	5/8 yd	3/4 yd
361-400	10	5/8 yd	7/8 yd
401-440	11	3/4 yd	1 yd

The Docking Zone Method

1. Join the binding strips with diagonal seams. This distributes the bulk of the seam, preventing a lump in the binding. (**Hint:** If the front and back of the fabric are the same — as with solids and batiks — press the strips of fabric in half *before* sewing them together. This makes it clear which side is the outside and will prevent you from mistakenly joining any pieces with the seam on the outside.)

2. With the back side of the binding fabric facing up, cut the starting end of the binding strip from upper right to lower left.

3. Press under 1/4" on this end, then press the binding strip in half lengthwise. The starting end now has a "docking zone."

4. Pin the binding strip to the front of the quilt with raw edges at the outside edge. Place the start of the binding strip about 6" from one corner. Start stitching just before the docking area and stitch completely over it. (**Hint:** Before sewing the entire strip, stitch a few inches and check that when you wrap the binding to the back side, the folded edge will cover the binding seam by just 1/8". If you need to adjust the width of the seam, do it by adjusting the needle position from side to side. This lets you keep the side of the foot along the edge of the fabric and will keep the width of the seam consistent.)

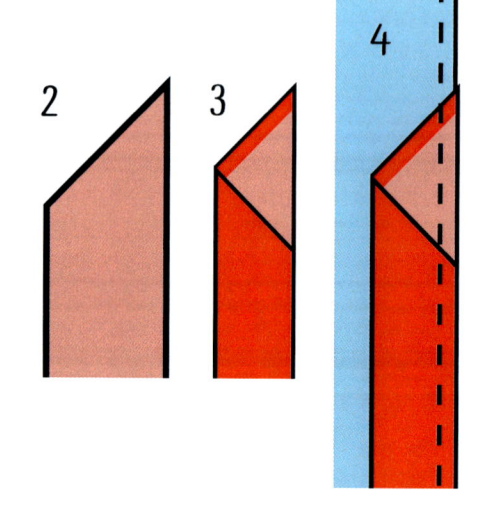

5. Sew the binding all the way around the quilt. Miter the binding strip at each corner.

6. To miter corners: Stitch toward the corner. Before you get there, finger-press the binding at a 45-degree angle (yellow line). Stop stitching exactly at this line.

7. Fold the binding up on a 45 degree angle at the corner, keeping the raw edges even with the next side of the quilt.

8. Fold the binding down, keeping the fold exactly at the top edge and the raw edges along the side of the quilt. Starting at the told, stitch over the binding strip and to the next corner. Repeat Steps 6-7-8 at each corner

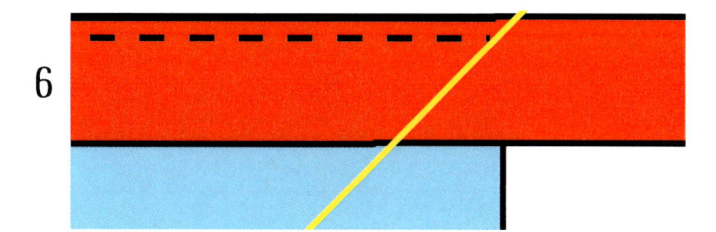

Joining the ends of the binding

9. When you come back to the docking zone, cut off excess binding strip just before the point where the seam crosses the hemmed edge of the strip.

10. Tuck the cut end of the binding strip under the folded edge of the docking zone. Stitch over the docking zone.

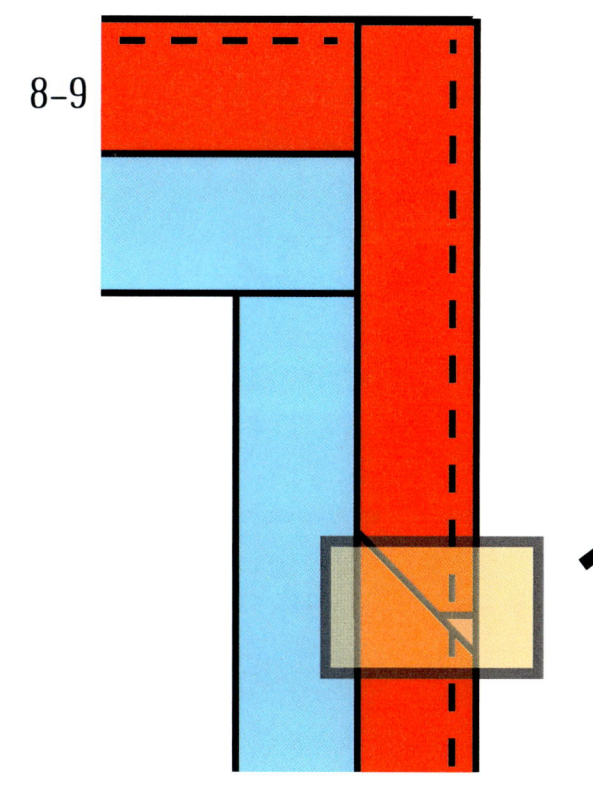

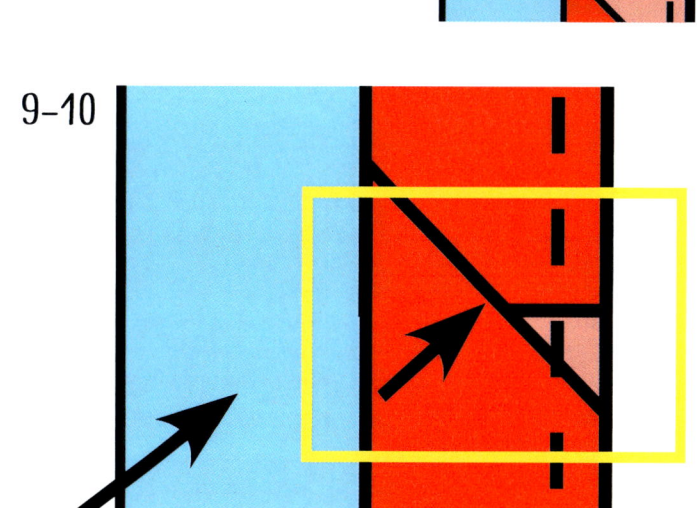

11. Turn the binding to the back of the quilt. At mitered corners, fold the binding so that the bulk on the back sits opposite of the bulk on the front. Use glue to hold the folded edge over the stitching line; set it with a hot dry iron.

12. Return to the front of the quilt and stitch-in-the-ditch along the edge of the binding. This will catch the folded edge on the back.

BINDING 67

Backing Yardages

Find your quilt dimensions on this chart for the amount of backing fabric needed for your quilt. Pay attention to the description in the column headed "Quilt Dimensions Relative to Bed Size"; this is where the table factors in, or leaves out, side drop, foot drop and pillow fold. Make sure you're using the correct size for how you want your quilt to fit on the bed — and on the human!

Note that the yardages do not take into account using the backing fabric in a particular direction — they are only the minimum needed. More fabric may be needed if you want to orient the design of a fabric one way or the other. It's a good idea to confirm yardage with a backing calculator. Check online (search "Backing Calculator for Quilts") or ask at your local quilt shop.

BED SIZE	BED HEIGHT	BED WIDTH	QUILT DIMENSIONS RELATIVE TO BED SIZE	FINISHED HEIGHT	FINISHED WIDTH	BACKING YARDS
CRIB / BABY	30	30		30	30	1 yd
	36	36		36	36	1-1/8 yds
	40	40		40	40	2-1/2 yds
	45	36		45	36	1-3/8 yds
	54	45		54	45	2-3/4 yds
TWIN	75	39	Top only below pillows	55	39	2-1/2 yds
			Top only	75	39	2-1/2 yds
			10" Drop on sides & foot only, no pillow wrap	85	59	5 yds
			10" Drop on sides & foot, 10" for pillow wrap	95	59	5-1/4 yds
DOUBLE	75	54	Top only below pillows	55	54	3-1/3 yds
			Top only	75	54	3-1/4 yds
			10" Drop on sides & foot only, no pillow wrap	85	74	5 yds
			10" Drop on sides & foot, 10" for pillow wrap	95	74	5-1/2 yds
QUEEN	80	60	Top only below pillows	60	60	3-5/8 yds
			Top only	80	60	4-3/4 yds
			10" Drop on sides & foot only, no pillow wrap	90	80	7 yds
			10" Drop on sides & foot, 10" for pillow wrap	100	80	7 yds

Tools for Building Strip Sets

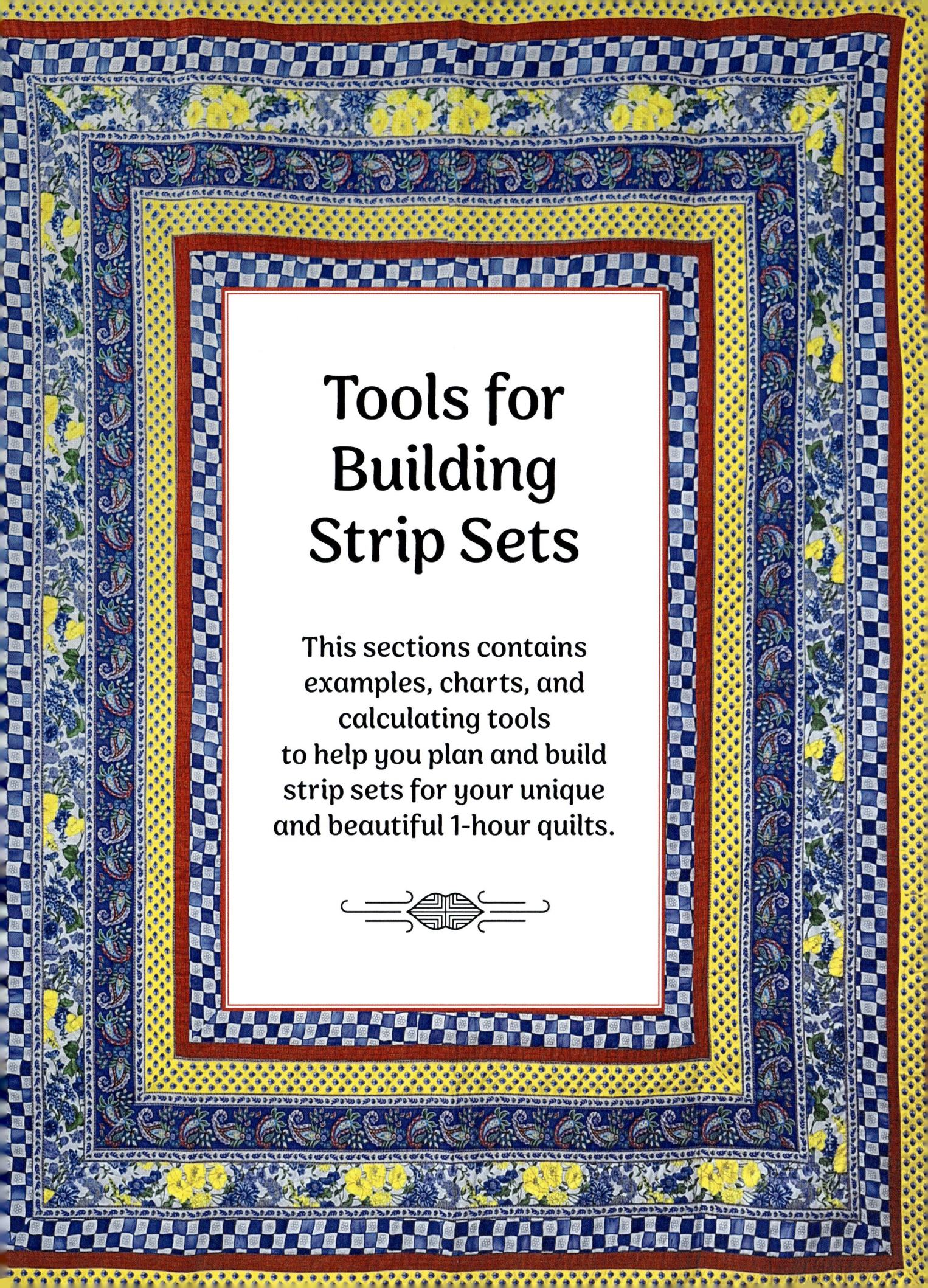

This sections contains examples, charts, and calculating tools
to help you plan and build strip sets for your unique and beautiful 1-hour quilts.

Strip Set Planning Tools

The tools on the next few pages will help you build strip sets for structurally solid and artistically beautiful Rectangle Box, Square Box or Diamond-in-the-Square quilts.

- The **Strip Set Planning Chart** will help you lay out the strip set, as you select fabrics, determine the order & width of strips, and plan how much you'll need.

- The **Component Strip Yardage Chart** on page 73 will help you determine how much fabric will be needed for each component strip, in any size quilt.

- The **Instructions** on page 74 will guide you through cutting, organizing and sewing your strip set.

- The **Examples** on (pages 75-79 will show you how I built strip sets for some of the quilts in this book. Learn from them, and if you wish, use them as patterns for your own quilts.

Strip Set Planning Chart Instructions

Use this chart to help you visualize, plan and organize a strip set. Work between laying the fabrics on the table top and coloring in the chart. As you experiment, take lots of pictures!

The width of the chart is 29", the size of the standard pattern. For a wider strip set, make copies, tape them together and write in your planned width.

Begin by filling in the top row with the Quilt Height, Quilt Width, Mother Strip Length and Mother Strip Width.

- Fill in the columns with the colors of your fabrics. For a 1" strip, fill in one column; for a 3" strip fill in three columns, etc. For 1/2", divide a column. See the example at right.

- When you've decided on your fabric placements, make a fresh copy of the table with the names, even swatches of each fabric in each column. Then fill in your measurements.

- Below each strip, on the row for Finished Strip Width (FSW), draw a box around the combined cells for that strip and write in the width of the strip. Add the strip widths across the table and fill in the MSW box. The total should equal the MSW box at the top of the chart.

- Below that, under the heading Cut Strip Widths (CSW), add 1/2" to each finished strip width and write that number in the box.

- Below that, number the strip.

- On the next two rows, write in the amount of fabric in inches and yards. Use the Component Strip Yardage Chart to calculate the yardage.

- On the last row, fill in the yardage needed for binding

As you cut and fabrics, refer back to the chart for sizes, and check each strip off as it is cut.

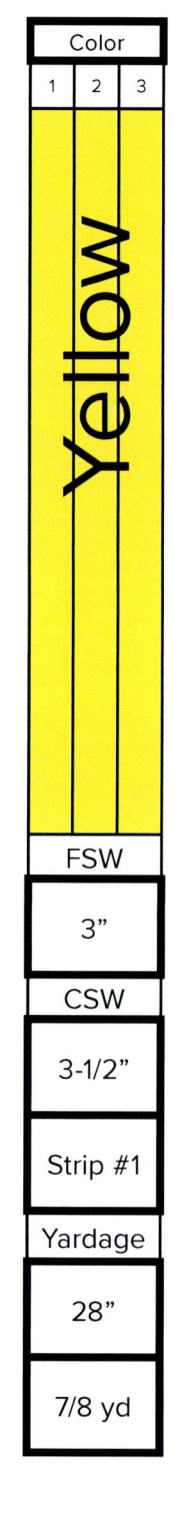

Color		
1	2	3

Yellow

FSW
3"

CSW
3-1/2"

Strip #1

Yardage
28"
7/8 yd

Strip Set Planning Chart

Quilt Height	Quilt Width	Mother Strip Length	Mother Strip Width

Colors

1	2	3	4	5	6	7	8	9	10	11	12	13	14	15	16	17	18	19	20	21	22	23	24	25	26	27	28	29

Finished Strip Widths (FSW) | MSW =

Cut Strip Widths (add 1/2" to Finished Width) (CSW)

Strip Numbers

Yardage Needed (from Component Strip Yardage Chart, page 72) | In Inches | In Yards

Binding Yardage (from table on page 66)

STRIP SET PLANNING CHART

Component Strip Yardage Chart Instructions

The **Component Strip Yardage Chart** gives you the amount of fabric you'll need for a component strip of any width within a strip set. The numbers are based on 42" width of fabric, which is based on 44" wide fabric minus selvages and seam allowances. The chart takes into account whether you cut fabric length of fabric or width of fabric. I have purposely NOT added in any extra fabric. This way, if you have a limited amount of a fabric, you'll know whether or not it is enough. If you are buying fabric, I suggest rounding up to the next 1/8 yard or even 1/4 yard if you want "insurance."

Instructions

▶ Write the Mother Strip Length in the upper left-hand corner of the table.

▶ Multiply MSL by Column C and fill in Column D for yardage needed to cut length of fabric.

▶ Divide MSL by 42 and fill in Column E for number of strips to cut width of fabric. The table at left below gives you a quick calculation.

▶ Multiply Column B by Column E for yardage needed to cut length of fabric. To convert inches to yards, divide by 36 and round up to the next 1/8 yard. The table at right below provides conversions from inches to decimals to fractions of a yard.

Should you cut LOF or WOF?

From an "on the grain" point of view, it doesn't matter whether you cut LOF or WOF. But there are two other determining factors to take into account: number of strips, and design direction.

▶ For strips longer than 42", you will have smallest number of pieces to join together if you cut LOF. For strips shorter than 42", you will have smallest number of pieces to join together if you cut WOF.

▶ If the design in the fabric dictates being cut one direction or the other, cut in the direction necessary for your quilt design.

▶ Follow the instructions in the chart between Columns D & E to determine which direction to cut.

MOTHER STRIP LENGTH (INCHES)	# WOF STRIPS
up to 42	1
43-84	2
84-126	3
127-168	4
169-210 (DITS Standard = 187")	5
211-252 (Square Box = 236")	6
253-294	7
295-336 (Rectangle Box = 324")	8
337-378	9
379-420	10
421-462	11
463-504	12

INCHES TO DECIMAL TO FRACTION CONVERSION CHART			
INCHES		DECIMALS	FRACTIONS OF A YARD
1 to 4-1/2		0 to 0.125	1/8
4-1/2 to 9		0.126 to 0.25	1/4
9 to 12		0.26 to 0.33	1/3
12 to 13-1/2		0.33 to 0.375	3/8
13-1/2 to 18		0.376 to 0.5	1/2
18 to 22-1/2		0.51 to 0.625	5/8
22-1/2 to 24		0.626 to 0.56	2/3
24 to 27		0.68 to 0.75	3/4
27 to 31-1/2		0.76 to 0.875	7/8

72   THE 1-HOUR QUILT TOP

Component Strip Yardage Chart

MSL =		IF CUTTING LOF			IF CUTTING WOF	
STRIP WIDTH		# OF LOF STRIPS YOU CAN CUT ACROSS WOF	YARDAGE NEEDED TO CUT LOF (INCHES & YDS)		# OF WOF STRIPS TO CUT	YARDAGE NEEDED TO CUT WOF (INCHES & YDS)
A	B	C	D	LOF or WOF?	E	F
FINISHED STRIP WIDTH	CUT WIDTH		Divide MSL by Column C		Divide MSL by 42	Col. B x Col. E = inches Divide by 36 for yards
20.5	21	2	MSL / 2 =	In order to cut the smallest number of pieces: Draw a line across Columns D & F where the value goes above 42". Lengths below 42" should be cut WOF unless the design of the fabric must be cut LOF unless the design in the fabric must be cut WOF. For examples see the Strip Set Yardage Charts for each standard pattern, found on pages 36, 50 & 58.	MSL / 42 = (Use the chart on the previous page for a quick calculation)	
20	20.5					
19.5	20					
19	19.5					
18.5	19					
18	18.5		/ 36 = yards			
17.5	18					
17	17.5					
16.5	17					
16	16.5					
15.5	16					
15	15.5					
14.5	15					
14	14.5	2 or 3				
13.5	14	3	MSL / 3 =			
13	13.5					
12.5	13		/ 36 = yards			
12	12.5					
11.5	12					
11	11.5					
10.5	11	3 or 4				
10	10.5	4	MSL / 4 =			
9.5	10		/ 36 = yards			
9	9.5					
8.5	9	4 or 5				
8	8.5	5	MSL / 5 =			
7.5	8		/ 36 = yards			
7	7.5					
6.5	7	6	MSL / 6 = / 36 = yards			
6	6.5					
5.5	6	7	MSL / 7 = / 36 = yards			
5	5.5					
4.5	5	8 or 9	MSL / 8 =			
4	4.5	9 or 10	MSL / 9 =			
3.5	4	11	MSL / 11 =			
3	3.5	12	MSL / 12 =			
2.5	3	14	MSL / 14 =			
2	2.5	16	MSL / 16 =			
1.5	2	21	MSL / 21 =			
1	1.5	28	MSL / 28 =			

Cutting, Organizing & Sewing a Strip Set

▶ Cut or tear each fabric into pieces for the component strips in the Strip Set Planning Chart.

▶ Wrap cut strips around a ruler to measure and store them. Label each strip with its position number and the length of the strip. Lay the wound strips in the order they will be assembled.

▶ Sew all the pieces of the same fabric end-to-end to make one component strip.

▶ HINT: If the fabric is directional (for example if it has animals that all face the same direction) be careful to keep all the strips facing the correct direction.

- Assemble the strips by sewing component strips into smaller groups, then into larger ones. Sew strip 1 to 2, then 3 to 4, etc. Next, join group 1-2 to group 3-4 to make 1-2-3-4 and so on. Build two halves of the strip set, then join the halves. Check the Strip Set Planning Chart frequently to make sure you have the strips in the right order!

- HINT: If one of the fabrics has a line that must be taken into account in construction, sew strips together with that line on top, so you can see where you are sewing.

Study the examples on the next several pages to help you build your own strip set and turn it into a beautiful quilt.

The strip set for the Provence quilt, cut, labeled and arranged in working order — ready to sew!

74   THE 1-HOUR QUILT TOP

Sample Quilts

On the next few pages, you'll find some of the sample quilts I made for this book, with the planning chart for each quilt. (If there's a bit of fuzziness or strange formatting, it is because these are screen shots of the actual spread sheets I created.)

Some quilts use border prints more than others, and some don't use them at all. With strip sets you're creating your own linear fabric so you can do anything you want.

Look at these, learn from them, use them as patterns if you wish. I hope they will inspire you to play, experiment with combinations, and make your own beautiful quilts!

The Provence Quilt

The strip set for this quilt is to the left.

This quilt began with a Provence-style striped fabric. I could have made the quilt with just that fabric, but it lacked variety, so I added fabrics: the yellow and lavender floral, the red solid, and the blue check.

I had only 4-1/4 yards of the Provence fabric. Because of how I had to cut it to build in seam allowance, I couldn't join strips to make longer strips. So, the mother strip was limited to 4-1/4 yards. That was enough to make a single Rectangle Box quilt a bit shorter than the standard pattern.

Since I was making a single quilt, the strip set had to be symmetrical. This one had 15 strips. When the strip set was assembled, it turned out to be 155" long and 31-1/2" wide. There was no excess length so I used the Half-and-Half construction method. The finished quilt is 77" x 62".

Time to make the quilt top

Tearing strips: about an hour
Sewing the strip set: 1 hour 45 minutes (about 7 minutes per strip)
Sewing the quilt: about an hour

MSW = 29"   MSL = 155"

Provence Quilt Colors

Colors (left to right): Yellow, Red, Blue Check, white stripe, Flowers, white stripe, Blue str, yellow, Red, Blue Check, Red, yellow, white stripe, Blue str, white stripe, Flowers, white stripe, Blue str, Blue Check, Red, Yellow

Finished Strip Widths

2.00 | 0.75 | 2.00 | 0.50 | 2.50 | 0.50 | 2.00 | 0.50 | 0.75 | 2.00 | 0.75 | 0.50 | 2.00 | 0.50 | 2.50 | 0.50 | 0.00 | 2.00 | 0.75 | 2.00

Total Mother Strip Width = 29.00

Cut Strip Widths

2.50 | 1.25 | 2.50 | 1.00 | 3.00 | 5.50 | 1.25 | 2.50 | 1.25 | 5.50 | 3.00 | 1.00/2.50 | 2.50 | 1.25 | 2.50

Strip #: 1, 2, 3, 4, 5, 6, 7, 8, 9, 10, 11, 12, 13, #, 15

Inches: 10, 5, 10, 4, 12, 22, 5, 10, 5, 22, 12, 10, 5, 10

Yds: 1/3, 1/4, 1/3, 1/4, 1/3, 1/4, 1/3, 1/4, 1/3, 1/3, 1/4, 1/3

Binding: Red: 7 strips 3" wide = 5/8 yard

The Autumn Quilts

This quilt includes a large leaf print, a small leaf print, a plaid, a green geometric, and a solid red. There are 9 strips. There's no border print, and there was enough of each fabric to make the full-size Rectangle Box standard pattern.

The mother strip was asymmetrical, 28-1/2" by 324" (9 yards) long. It made two sister quilts shown here, finished size 57" x 80".

Half & Half construction worked fine since the unstructured designs of the fabric could be broken across the end triangles.

Time to make both quilt tops

Tearing strips: about an hour
Sewing the strip set: 2 hours 15 minutes
(9 strips, about 15 minutes per strip)
Sewing each quilt top: about an hour

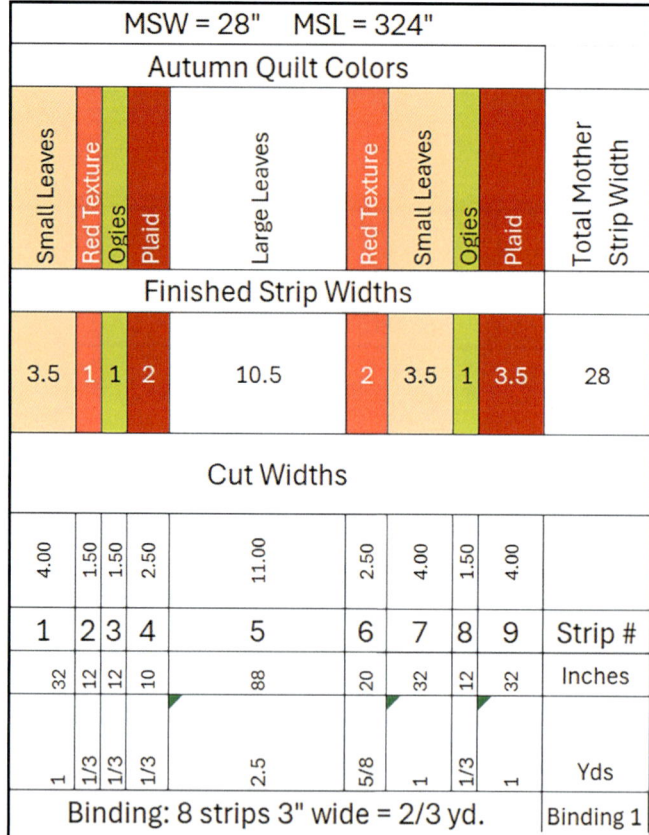

Autumn Quilt Colors

MSW = 28"   MSL = 324"

Small Leaves	Red Texture	Ogies	Plaid	Large Leaves	Red Texture	Small Leaves	Ogies	Plaid	Total Mother Strip Width

Finished Strip Widths

| 3.5 | 1 | 1 | 2 | 10.5 | 2 | 3.5 | 1 | 3.5 | 28 |

Cut Widths

4.00	1.50	1.50	2.50	11.00	2.50	4.00	1.50	4.00	
1	2	3	4	5	6	7	8	9	Strip #
32	12	12	10	88	20	32	12	32	Inches
1	1/3	1/3	1/3	2.5	5/8	1	1/3	1	Yds

Binding: 8 strips 3" wide = 2/3 yd.   Binding 1

76   THE 1-HOUR QUILT TOP

The Garden Quilts

A bright garden and butterflies come together in this quilt, along with leaves, yellow gingham, a subtle red strips, and a green lattice print. There are 7 strips in the set.

The mother strip was asymmetrical, 29-1/2" by 324" (9 yards) long. It made two sister quilts shown here, finished size 58" x 80".

Although the garden fabric had some large structural elements, flowers and foliage softened the design so that the Half & Half method was suitable for construction.

Time to make both quilt tops

Tearing strips: about an hour
Sewing the strip set: 1 hour 45 minutes
(7 strips, about 15 minutes per strip)
Sewing each quilt top: about an hour

	MSW = 29" MSL = 324"
	Garden Quilt
Dk Green Leaves	Red	Butterflies	Green ogies	Garden fabric Printed across WOF 8 repeats = 352 linear inches	Red	Yellow gingham	Mother Strip Width
	Finished Widths
5.00	1.25	3.50	1.5	11.50	1.25	5.00	29.00
	Cut Widths
5.50	1.75	4.00	2.00	12.00	1.75	5.50	
1	2	3	4	5	6	7	Strip #
	LOF needed
44"	14"	32"	16"	96"	14"	44"	inches
1.25	1	0.875	1	2.67	1	1.25	yards
	Binding: 8 strips 3" wide = 2/3 yd.

AUTUMN QUILTS & GARDEN QUILTS

The Blue Daisy Quilts

I had less than 2 yards of the blue daisy border print, but there were four repeats of the stripe across width of fabric, so I separated the repeats and sewed them end-to-end into a strip 7-1/2 yards long. This was the maximum mother strip length.

Other fabrics were two shades of blue, two shades of green, and two shades of brown. Using different shades of the same color gave variety while staying within the color palette of the key fabric.

I chose to make Square Box quilts. The mother strip divided into four lengths of 68", so the strip set width was 34", half the sides of the square. The strip set was asymmetrical, with 13 component strips. Finished size of the larger quilt is 67" square.

When I cut the mother strip into triangles, I made the mistake of not marking them out before I began to make sure they all fit. I ended up short on the last triangle, so I had to cut down three other triangles to match it. This made the second quilt top smaller.

Time to make both quilt tops

Tearing strips: about an hour
Sewing the strip set: 2 hours 15 minutes
(13 strips, about 15 minutes per strip)
Sewing each quilt top: about an hour (plus time to re-cut the triangles in the smaller top)

MSW = 34"   MSL = 270" (7.5 yds)

Blue Daisy Quilt Colors

Blue	Brown	Check	Brown	Green	Daisies	Blue	Brown	Tan	Brown	Woven	Brown	Check	Total Mother Strip Width

Finished Strip Widths

| 3 | 1 | 4 | 1 | 3 | 7 | 3.5 | 1 | 2 | 1 | 3 | 1 | 3.5 | 34 |

Cut Widths

3.50	1.50	4.50	1.50	3.50	7.50	3.50	1.50	2.50	1.50	3.50	1.50	4.00	13 strips
1	2	3	4	5	6	7	8	9	10	11	12	13	Strip #
24.50	10.50	31.50	10.50	24.50	52.50	24.50	10.50	17.50	10.50	24.50	10.50	28.00	Inches
0.68	0.29	0.88	0.29	0.68	1.46	0.68	0.29	0.49	0.29	0.68	0.29	0.78	Yds

Binding: Red: 7 strips 3" wide = 5/8 yard

78   THE 1-HOUR QUILT TOP

The Plaid Diamond Quilt

The focal print of this quilt is not a border print but a multicolor woven plaid. I had very limited amounts of both the plaid and the stripe, so there was only enough for one small quilt. Using the fabrics in a DITS quilt made them look as though I had a lot more of them; cut into all eight triangles, each fabric appears eight times in the quilt.

There were so many color options with this plaid that the design challenge was which colors NOT to use. I played with the fabrics in several sessions and took LOTS of photos before I finally settled on this combination.

Finished size is 36" square.

Time to make the quilt top

I didn't keep track of the various stages of this quilt, but I did make the whole top in one evening, from cutting the strips to assembling the triangles.

MSW = 12.75"							MSL = 125" (3.5 yds)
Plaid Quilt Colors							
Plaid	Gold	Orange	Turquoise	Stripe	Coral	magenta	Total Mother Strip Width
5.5	1	0.75	1	2	2	1	12.75
Cut Widths							
6.00	1.50	1.25	1.50	2.50	2.00	1.50	
1	2	3	4	5	6	7	Strip #
18.00	4.50	3.75	4.50	7.50	6.00	4.50	Inches
0.50	0.13	0.10	0.13	0.21	0.17	0.13	Yds
Binding: Fuchsia 4 strips = 1/3 yd							

Now it's YOUR turn to create!

Mother Strip Length Inches to Yards Conversion

Tables within each pattern give you the mother strip length and yardages for any size using that pattern. This table is a universal and simplified conversion tool: if your mother strip is a certain length in inches, it will tell you how long that is in yards.

MOTHER STRIP LENGTH (USE THIS NUMBER IN THE STRIP YARDAGE CHART)	LENGTH (IN YARDS) OF WHOLE-CLOTH FABRIC (ROUNDED UP TO NEAREST 1/8 YARD)
424	12
404	11-1/4
384	10-2/3
364	10-1/8
356	10
348	9-2/3
340	9-1/2
332	9-1/4
324	9
316	8-7/8
308	8-5/8
300	8-1/3
292	8-1/8
284	8
276	7-2/3
268	7-1/2
260	7-1/4
252	7
244	6-7/8
236	6-5/8
228	6-1/3
220	6-1/8
212	6
204	5-2/3
196	5-1/2
188	5-1/4
180	5
172	4-7/8
164	4-5/8
156	4-1/3
148	4-1/8
140	4

Resources

How About a Class?

I have taught in-person quilting classes in lots of places around the world since 2008. And I still do, occasionally. But more and more (because I ain't getting any younger!) I teach online via recorded video classes that you can access anytime. And, sometimes I also do live online events.

To see my calendar and my online classes, visit my website and follow the tabs at the top to go to "Classes & Calendar" or "Shop Online."

www.RaNaeMerrillQuilts.com

If you would like to get notifications about new events, sign up for my email on the "Contact" tab.

I'd love to see you in a class some time!

Where to get Hobbs Heirloom Fusible Batting

I'll tell you what I always tell my students: buy from your local quilt shop whenever you can. *Even if it costs a little bit more.* Ask if they can special order this batting for you. Remember: LQS's provide SO much more than fabric. They are your happy place, your quilting club house. They help you, answer questions, give you hugs and almost always have some form of chocolate on hand. Appreciate them by shopping with them.

I don't have a quilt shop in NYC that stocks this batting (they are really small and there's not a lot of space for bulky things like batting), and also, I'm not home very much. So I buy my quilting supplies from whatever LQS is near wherever I am. If I can't get my batting from an LQS, then I order online.

I like Hancock's of Paducah.

www.hancocks-paducah.com

Connecting Threads is also a reliable source.

www.connectingthreads.com

Fabric Companies

Here is a list of some of the bigger fabric companies where I have found border prints. The list is not complete, but it's a place to start.

Andover Fabrics	**Maywood**
Art Gallery Fabrics	**Moda**
Benartex	**Northcott**
Blank Quilting	**Quilting Treasures**
Clothworks	**Riley Blake**
Free Spirit	**Studio E (Jaftex)**
Hoffman Fabrics	**Timeless Treasures**
In the Beginning	**Windham Fabrics**
Kaufman Fabrics	

For more, visit the Hancock's of Paducah website and click on "Shop by Brand" for a full list of fabric manufacturers.

My Socials

Hashtag for this book: #1hourquilt

Insta: ranaequilts, freemotionmasteryinamonth

FB: RaNae Merrill Quilt Design, RaNae Merrill, Free-Motion Mastery in a Month

YouTube: RaNae Merrill (@RMQDNYC)
Free Motion Mastery in a Month (@free-motionmasteryinamonth4411)

A Moment of Peace and Awe (@AMomentofPeaceandAwe)

If You Find an Error

I try VERY hard when writing a book to get everything right so you can confidently rely on what I've written. That said, I'm also human, and sometimes I goof. So if you find an error, please let me know. Just please, be kind. You can email me at

ranae@ranaemerrillquilts.com

More Books from RaNae Merrill

Available at www.RaNaeMerrillQuilts.com and Amazon

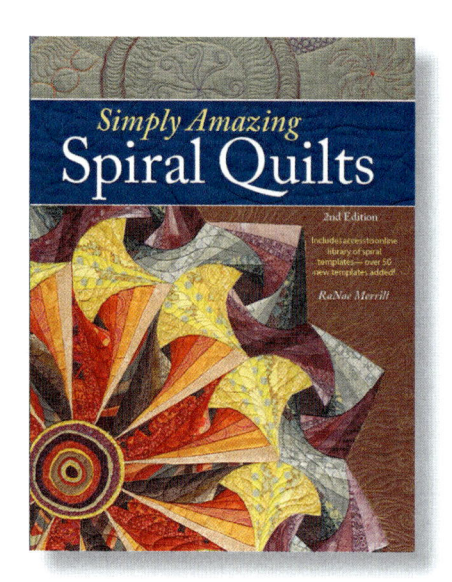

Simply Amazing Spiral Quilts

My best-selling first book on spiral quilt design teaches you to make four types of spirals and variations on them. Then, explore a wide variety of spiral quilt settings. Includes 5 projects and an online library of hundreds of spiral blocks.

160 pages, $40.00

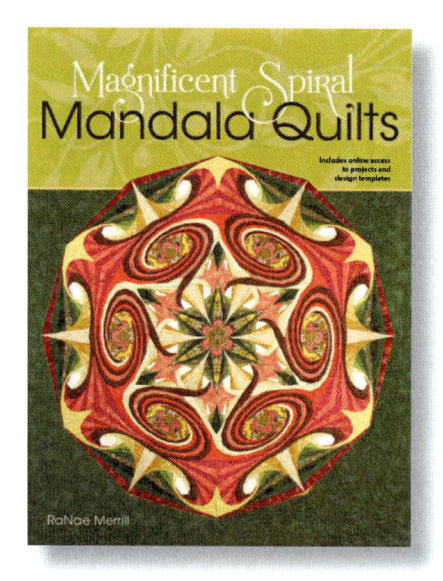

Magnificent Spiral Mandala Quilts

These kaleidoscopic mandala quilts are designed with mirrors and dry-erase markers, and sewn with a simple variation of the Log Cabin block. Photos of over 50 exquisite quilts make this a must-have just for the eye candy! Includes 6 complete patterns.

160 pages, $40.00

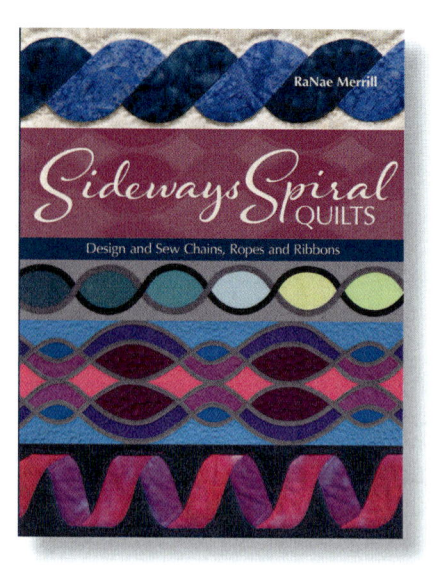

Sideways Spiral Quilts

Think DNA, licorice twists, ropes, cheese sticks — all spirals seen from the side. Learn simple methods for incorporating chains, ropes and ribbons into your quilt designs. Six projects and dozens of photographs will spark your creativity.

164 pages, $40.00

Free-Motion Mastery in a Month

Build machine-quilting skills and confidence day-by-day with unique movement exercises — from straight lines to feathers! RaNae's 25 years experience as a piano teacher inspired this highly effective learning system for all types of sewing machine.

176 pages $40.00

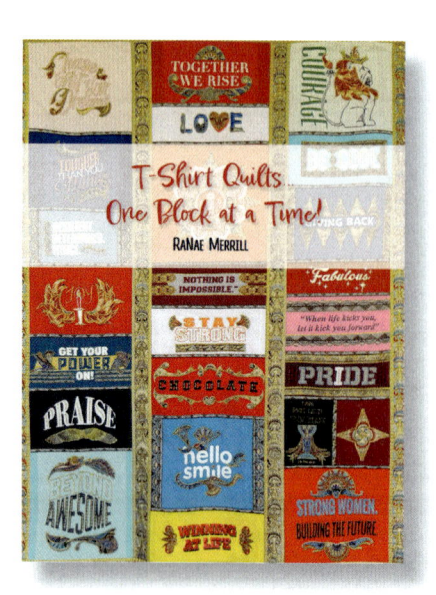

T-Shirt Quilts One Block at a Time!

This quilt-as-you-go approach to making T-shirt quilts is fun and easy! Quilt each shirt yourself on your domestic sewing machine. There's no big, stretchy top to deal with, and you don't even need to plan the layout in advance.

98 pages $25.00

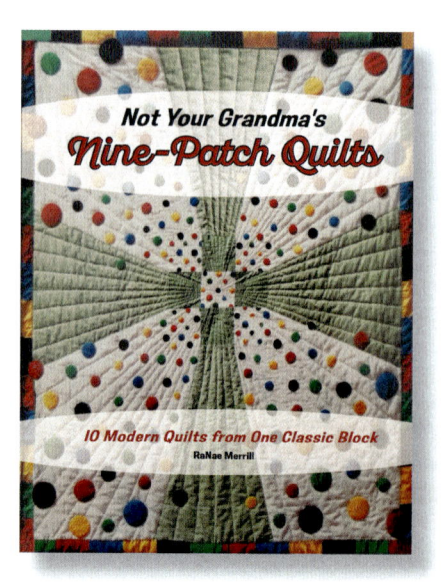

Not Your Grandma's Nine-Patch Quilts

Nearly 50 years ago, I found some 9-patch blocks that my grandma had left in an old chest. As my nieces and nephews were born, I incorporated the blocks into these unique and modern baby quilts. Includes 10 patterns.

118 pages $30.00

82   THE 1-HOUR QUILT TOP